MUSICIANS
IN CAMERA

MUSICIANS IN CAMERA

PHOTOGRAPHS BY LAELIA GOEHR
TEXT BY JOHN AMIS

WITH A FOREWORD BY SIR YEHUDI MENUHIN

BLOOMSBURY

First published in Great Britain 1987
Text copyright © 1987 by John Amis
Photographs copyright © 1987 by Laelia Goehr
Design copyright © 1987 by Bloomsbury Publishing Ltd

Bloomsbury Publishing Ltd, 2 Soho Square, London W1V 5DE

British Library Cataloguing in Publication Data

Goehr, Laelia
    Musicians in camera : a private view of
    the world's greatest composers, conductors and performers
    1. Musicians — Portraits
    I. Title   II. Amis, John
    780'.92'2   ML87

ISBN 0-7475-0042-8

Designed by Roy Williams and Laurence Bradbury
Assisted by Sarah Collins
Phototypeset by SX Composing Ltd, Rayleigh, Essex
Printed and bound in Italy by Amilcare Pizzi Spa, Milan

CONTENTS

to Gillian Catto
who, in the course of happy afternoons at the
Catto Gallery, turned the idea of the book
into a reality

FOREWORD

In some ways, perhaps, music could be described as the flowing moment, and it is a rare gift to be able, even momentarily, to focus upon that moment and hold it in a kind of suspension. There are those who say the camera lies, or that it never lies: this paradox is put severely to the test when the camera confronts musicians at work. Or should I say at play? Because the difference is difficult to distinguish.

Interrupted moments, divisions of time, measures musicians must observe with an almost martial scrupulousness, hurry by. How do you manage to arrest and freeze the moment, while at the same time conveying to those who look at your photography that the moment is not frozen or arrested but flows onwards? That for me is the test of an exceptional photographer. There are answers to my questions in these pictures by Laelia Goehr, where making music is caught on the wing. A difficult achievement, for musicians at work simply cannot acknowledge, or recognise, the fact that somebody wants them to stop long enough to register the moment.

Seldom have I seen images which flow with the music and the musicians in quite such harmony. Laelia Goehr possesses the sensitivity to show us as we are, and were, and, with many of these unforgettable artists, will continue to be – in full pursuit of that perfection to which all musicians aspire and which all honest musicians acknowledge to be unattainable. If there is any one thing that I can say about these photographs which so move me, it is their recognition of the curious never-ending delight in the unattainable, and the sheer joy of sometimes approaching it. In music, fleeting, evanescent and fugitive as it is, this is a real achievement, for which one is deeply grateful.

There can be few people who look more deeply behind the scenes than Laelia Goehr. Perhaps, being the mother of one of Britain's most distinguished composers, she understands the delicacy and the difficulty of capturing instants from this onward flow of musical life and history, which might otherwise pass before one knew it. Most people in the audience look with their ears. It is wonderful that someone looks with her ears *and* her eyes, and is so attuned as to be able to listen, and look, and make us see – ourselves!

Music is difficult to picture; it is meant to be heard. Words fail in the midst of music and if it is unusual to find pictures as evocative as these then it is probably as difficult to find words to match, to accompany them, with the appropriate rhythm and harmony. John Amis accompanies the photographs in this extraordinary historical documentary of our musical life and times with a delightfully witty and erudite text. This is one of those happy occasions when words, pictures and music genuinely belong together.

This is the *theatre* of music – up on the stage among the members of the orchestra, the conductor and the soloist a drama, or a comedy – or sometimes when things are going badly, a tragedy – is being played out. In Laelia Goehr's photographs we, the players, have dropped our masks, and our audience sees us without the benefit of props and make-up, as we really are.

YEHUDI MENUHIN
July 1987

7

IGOR STRAVINSKY

B. 1882 ORANIENBAUM, D. 1971 NEW YORK

The greatest composer of this century – and the smallest? First and foremost a Russian, he left at the Revolution, became a French citizen in 1934 and an American in 1945. When the news of Pearl Harbour came through, his first angry question was 'Where will I go now?'

Typical of this century, Stravinsky was a stylistic time-traveller. He began as a pupil of Rimsky-Korsakov, and ended emulating, but adding his own gloss to, the Second Viennese School style, the music of Webern in particular. In between came his best music, none more popular than the first three ballets he composed for the Diaghilev company: *Firebird* 1910, *Petrushka* 1911 and *The Rite of Spring* 1913. In those four years he proved himself a master: *Firebird* is a kind of apotheosis of nineteenth-century Russian nationalism; *Petrushka* takes in not only Russia but also the latest French developments of his friends Debussy and Ravel then steps beyond them; and the *Rite* was the great seminal work for the future. Quite rightly, the *Rite* caused a riot at its première in Paris. Stravinsky at 31 became world famous, bogeyman and leader of the avant-garde.

Stravinsky never wrote a second anything; just as each of the three major ballets differed (and because of copyright difficulties, Stravinsky did not receive performing rights on them, a rankling wound throughout his life), so every work that followed was *sui generis*. After the unprecedentedly large orchestra of the *Rite*, Stravinsky scaled down to the chamber ensemble for *The Soldier's Tale*, incorporating jazz elements. The next Diaghilev ballet was *Pulcinella* based on Pergolesi's music. The pattern continued: A *Piano Concerto* in the neo-classical idiom, piano solo works that recalled Weber and Beethoven, a 'white' ballet *Apollo* that flirted with Tchaikovsky, an opera-oratorio *Oedipus Rex* with a text in Latin, as was the text of the *Symphony of Psalms*, a Haydnesque *Symphony in C*, a Bachian *Violin*

Concerto.

Some loved the *dernier cri* aspect of this art – Stravinsky leading musical fashion: the critics were mostly left behind bewailing One Damn Thing After Another, or comparing Stravinsky's about-faces profitably with Picasso's. The extraordinary fact was that, no matter where he turned or what he borrowed or imitated, Stravinsky remained Stravinsky, inevitably and inexorably himself, his musical fingerprints unmistakable. To be sure, other composers imitated him, but they lacked his authority, his ritual and spiritual qualities. His textures were elegant, his rhythms compulsive with their displaced beat and accents. His melodies were not the most expressive part of his music but there was always present in his music a sense of theatre

and a discernible dramatic structure. He once famously said that, like his nose, music could express nothing, but, although he tried to prevent musicians from putting expression *into* his music, his music was never *without* expressive qualities (and just look at that nose of his!)

Stravinsky liked the best things in life: food, drink, people, artists; he knew and/or worked with Nijinsky, Cocteau, Picasso, Bakst, Fokine, Balanchine, Cocteau, Eliot, Dylan Thomas, and Auden (who wrote the libretto for Stravinsky's 1951 opera *The Rake's Progress*). Stravinsky continued to flirt with jazz – *Ebony Concerto* was composed for Woody Herman – and finally with serialism, the finest example of his work in that genre being the enchanting ballet *Agon*.

Desperately short of money following the Revolution, Stravinsky became a performer to earn, first as pianist, later as conductor. He had a reputation for being as mean with dollars as he was with musical intervals, once planning no less than three concerts on his birthday (which he was quite entitled to do, owing to the difference of twelve days between Western and Russian calendars, and the fact that Russia made 1900 a leap year when the rest of the world did not).

Stravinsky married twice. In his later years he also had living in his house an American secretary/amanuensis called Robert Craft; with Craft's help several books were concocted giving us much of the wit, wisdom and experience of the great Igor. Chronicled in these books is the triumphant tour of 1962, the sole occasion when Stravinsky returned to the land of his birth.

He died at the age of 89 and his body was buried in Venice, near to Diaghilev's, as he wished.

ARTUR RUBINSTEIN

B. 1887 LÓDŹ, D. 1982 GENEVA

A *bon viveur* – as soon as he came onto the platform you felt that here was a man of the world; he had charm, he had presence, he had style. He might move you with his playing of Chopin – the mazurkas especially had the right feel; his Spanish music or Villa-Lobos was authentic, glittering and passionate; the selection from *Petrushka* that Stravinsky transcribed especially for him was brilliant; his Brahms civilized the hairy old Hamburger; his Mozart could be touching. When it came to Beethoven, you felt that Rubinstein was a *Les Adieux* pianist rather than an *Appassionata* one, more elegance than drama, more lightning than thunder. With Michelangeli or Richter you suspect that the artist might have a solitary meal after the recital, perhaps reading Nietzsche or Turgeniev, whereas you *knew* that Rubinstein would be at the Savoy Grill or perhaps at some grand house, with the best wines, the best cigars and the best people, discoursing in one of the eight languages he spoke fluently, regaling the company with witty and well-told *histoires*. His English accent was broken but posh, acquired no doubt during those years when being a pianist meant society drawing-rooms and weekends with the nobility, as much as concert halls, practising and travelling.

Rubinstein had a prodigious memory, wonderful for the music that was stored in his brain but rather tiresome when it came to the second of the two vast volumes of autobiography that he published late in life, because the author spared us nothing. As so often with showbiz biogs, the struggle interests, success bores. It emerged from the books that, after the prodigy's triumphs – début under the baton of Joachim in Berlin – the virtuoso took life easy in his twenties; at forty or so he finally married a delightful lady who took him in hand and made him a conscientious musician and family man, to such good effect that Rubinstein matured as an artist; he recorded and gave concerts until his late eighties.

LORD BENJAMIN BRITTEN

B. 1913 LOWESTOFT, D. 1976 ALDEBURGH

Ben was a competitive chap; he liked to be the best, he liked applause. Generally he *was* the best: at composing, or playing the piano, or conducting, or running the Aldeburgh Festival; he was a good driver of fast cars; he played tennis well (placing the ball as shrewdly and idiosyncratically as he would a note), croquet and even Happy Families (although one Christmas time Shostakovich — on a visit — was allowed to win). On the other hand Ben admired people who did things as well as himself, or did them in slightly different fields, as witness his duets with Richter or Rostropovich (for whom he composed a *Sonata*, three *Suites* and a massive *Symphony for Cello and Orchestra*). There has never in musical history been a love-match that has produced so much music as Ben wrote for Peter Pears: at least eight song-cycles and ten operas (from *Peter Grimes* in 1945 to *Death in Venice* in 1973). The preponderance of subject matter relating to the corruption of innocence and sympathy for the underdog must surely have had a lot to do with Ben's own experience, mainly in relation to being a homosexual.

Britten believed his task was to write music for the living. Like Mozart, most of his music was composed with certain voices or instrumentalists in mind. He would tailor the music for their particular voices, for example, knowing which were the best notes in the voice, wide intervals or narrow, which parts of the voice 'spoke' best, was the singer better at quick or slow music; all the individuality of that person is so much encapsulated in music which amounts to a portrait of their particular voice. The music written especially for Fischer-Dieskau, Vyvyan, Baker, Vishnevskaya, Mandikian, Ferrier, and Pears above all, still sounds like those singers even when others perform it. Britten also knew exactly how any instrumentalist was going to produce any note he wrote down for him or her: which finger, method of blowing, bowing, striking, pedalling, which string; you ignore his written indications at the performance's peril. (By the way, none of this means that his music is easy to perform; it is always *possible* though.) There is but one single example of his making a boo-boo, and he could afford to laugh about it — a low piccolo note in *Billy Budd* which is off the instrument.

Ben was a fascinating person to be with; a rather melting upper-middle-class accent, the manner of a diffident prep-school master (clothes to match — a sports coat and grey bags *à l'anglaise*). He could charm anybody if he wanted something or liked you; but he could also easily take a dislike to you. Favourites could be snubbed and badly hurt over a bad performance or imagined slight. For years Ben would not conduct the London Symphony because one day a couple of double basses laughed at something in a newspaper and he thought they were laughing at his conducting.

His conducting was penetratingly good; his performances of Mozart or Schumann sounded as if the music had just been composed, not only with the ink still fresh but with the heart of the music still laid bare. His piano playing was again from the core of the music out, with orchestral colour in everything. His sympathy with his partner was infinite, the same when he was conducting for others.

Perhaps Ben had one skin less than most of us. That might account for the extreme sensitivity. Perhaps the best of his music is inspired by words. Not only are they impeccably set but set with an imagination that enhances and re-creates the writer's spirit, style and imagery. He often chose words that you would think would be impossible to set or that would be destroyed in the setting. Strangely enough, except in the wordless *Prince of the Pagodas*, there is no love duet.

I believe he turned down a knighthood, but was later awarded the Order of Merit and the first peerage ever given to a musician.

SIR MICHAEL TIPPETT

B. 1905 LONDON

Michael Tippett has an extraordinary ebullience of spirit. He has a poetic awareness of nature, people, ideas and things that goes very deep in his music. Sometimes all this can be apparent when you talk to him or read his words, but at other times some of the thinking can seem to flit without too much reason from one thing to another. But the music makes the connection and explains all. In fact the music is impossible to get near to in words, which is as it should be. To paraphrase what Copland once said: music is a precise language but I cannot tell you what any particular piece means, which is why it is music and not words.

Michael's confidence in himself is exceptional, always was; he hasn't preserved any music of his before parts of his first *String Quartet*, written when he was thirty – pretty late for a composer. Then he managed to analyse his own psyche and suddenly the music came out straight. With no income except from schoolmastering and running choirs and amateur orchestras, Michael got the habit of living simply; and he is the same today in his eighties, give or take the odd glass of champagne and a penchant for airline tickets to exotic places.

Tippett's ideals ran close to Britten's in the Forties; they were both pacifists. I once went with Ben to visit Michael who was serving a three-month sentence in Wormwood Scrubs prison – that was in World War II when conscientious objectors were thus punished. In addition, they both adored Purcell and Dowland, were fed up with Brahms and too much folkery, represented something new as opposed to Walton, and Vaughan Williams and so on, so their names were often bracketed together. But their ways and music were entirely different. Tippett is more like Beethoven in wrestling with the unborn notes and shapes, not writing for particular performers, and not always knowing how a certain work will turn out or be performed, let alone (like Britten) knowing which finger will play which note on which string (or whatever).

Tippett directed the Bath Festival successfully between 1969 and '74, and he sometimes conducts his own music to advantage, but on the whole he sits at home and composes – rather slowly.

He works hard, gets fractious if interrupted, but is great company when his task is over for the day. He never plays the piano for fun (it wouldn't *be* much fun) but he loves *Dallas* and, until his eyesight deteriorated, was a murderous player of demon patience.

How marvellous it is that this musical prophet has been honoured in his own lifetime! And in a local, social sense, he has been honoured by his own country – a knighthood and the Order of Merit.

SIR WILLIAM WALTON

B. 1902 OLDHAM, D. 1983 ISCHIA

'There's this pale chap, with pale hair and pale manner and yet his music is full of guts and blood and spunk and sheer venom' (Laurence Olivier talking about his friend William Walton).

They first met at the time of Walton's first *Symphony*, which is full of all those qualities (except paleness) and has one movement that lives up to its unique marking *Presto con malizia*. For one season this work emulated Schubert's in being *Unfinished* and was performed that way. The composer had got stuck and the finale would not emerge until he had found another girlfriend, the first one having inspired in turn a first movement of incredible turbulence, a scherzo of malice and an adagio of passionate lyricism. Mind you, knowing him over many years, I learned to take anything that William said with great quantities of salt. Out of a mixture of laziness, humour, Lancastrian caution and bloodymindedness he would say anything that came into his head, even if it contradicted what he had previously said in answer to the same question.

'When I was at Oxford I spent quite a time looking for geniuses but they were rather thin on the ground just after World War I; but I did find William and brought him up to London to meet my brother and sister, Osbert and Edith' (Sacheverell Sitwell talking about his friend Walton). Son of a choirmaster, William had become a chorister at Christ Church, Oxford, and later became a young undergraduate there. Instead of taking any examinations, he went to live in London with Osbert and Edith, even growing to *look* like a Sitwell. He was persuaded to write some music for some of Edith's experimental poetic exercises in rhythms; the result was *Façade*, a work that in 1922 brought the twenty-year-old a riotous première and some kudos but, for quite a time, no publisher.

At Salzburg, four English ladies dressed in virginal white played his *String Quartet* but subsided through the floor during the perfor-

mance; the work sank just as surely. However, Walton's *Viola Concerto* (1927), his biblical cantata *Belshazzar's Feast* (1931) and his *Symphony* (1934/5) put him firmly on the map. During the Forties he wrote some of the best scores the cinema has known: *Henry V*, *Hamlet* and, in 1955, *Richard III* (all directed by Olivier).

In 1948 Willie (*Sir* William in '51, Order of Merit in '68) went with his Argentinian bride to live in Ischia where he composed a late-Romantic opera, *Troilus and Cressida*. He was upset that it was rather a flop and by the fact that few listeners thought that his post-war music had quite the zap and sap of the earlier music. Certain creative artists seem continually to tackle new problems whereas others, like Walton, seem only to find alternative solutions to old problems. Who knows, perhaps his stories about the inspiring love affairs of his bachelor days were true . . . ? Never mind, Walton's best is some of England's finest.

One story that illustrates his sense of humour. (But first you have to know that in 1952 when Bax died, Walton was miffed that he was passed over as a choice for being Master of the Queen's Music in favour of Sir Arthur Bliss.) A few months before he died Walton passed out and was clinically dead for some minutes. By the bedside later, a friend asked him: 'William, what was it like on the other side; *were* they playing late Beethoven?'

'No, at first it was mercifully quiet; and then they started playing a fanfare, not one of mine actually; Bliss, I suppose.'

DARIUS MILHAUD

B. 1892 AIX-EN-PROVENCE, D. 1974 GENEVA

'I am a Frenchman from Provence, and by religion a Jew' is how his autobiography opens. The first time I met Milhaud (he pronounced his name 'Mee-Oh' by the way) he was drinking a cup of coffee as in Laelia's picture of him, but he was scowling and snapping at his interviewer:

'I notice that in the manuscript of your latest orchestral work, opus 414, there is not a single mistake or correction; I can't even write a letter without corrections.'

'Perhaps that tells more about you than me; next question.'

'Is this latest work composed in sonata form?'

'There is no such thing as sonata form so that is a very stupid question.' Ouch!

To be fair, I think the *Maître* was having a bad morning and he did suffer from bad health; in the picture you can see the strange texture of his skin, pachydermatous, so that I believe he could not perspire; he also had rheumatism so badly that he had to use a wheelchair . . . *except* when he went to teach in Colorado at Aspen where the high altitude suited him so well that he could get up and walk a bit.

The next time I interviewed Milhaud, he was sweetness itself, maybe because I was making a TV film about his old friend, Poulenc, by then dead for nearly ten years. Milhaud said he felt sad coming back to Paris because every time the telephone rang he thought 'it was going to be dear Francis, but of course now it never will be.' I asked him about the unevenness of Poulenc's output and he would not hear of it: 'I loved Francis like a brother; all his works are part of him; I love them too.' Perhaps this attitude was similar to his feelings about his own works; there are 441 of them with opus numbers. No more than a dozen of them get played; it is always *La Création du monde, Suite Provençale, Le boeuf sur le toit, Scaramouche*. I know at least another ten marvellous ones but the weight of so many uninspired churned-out ones is an inhibiting factor.

When we had finished our interview I asked Milhaud if there was anything he would like from London. 'Yes, I would dearly love to see a score of that remarkable motet by that Elizabethan composer Thomas Tallis; it is written in forty real parts. I have written some complicated counterpoint in my music but nothing as much as forty.'

I sent the score to him and received a charming letter from him. He died a few weeks later.

SIR ADRIAN BOULT

B. 1889 CHESTER, D. 1983 TUNBRIDGE WELLS

'It is an unfortunate thing that the conductor's job, even when we over-exert ourselves as most of us do, looks quite easy and, what's more, glamorous: for, like playing the organ, it gives a great sense of power,' wrote Sir Adrian in his book *Thoughts on Conducting*. Typical, of course, that he writes 'as most of us do' because *he* didn't. Boult was an incredibly modest man. Not modest for music, only about himself. He believed that conducting was about integrity and doing what the composer wanted, which included *finding out* what the composer wanted – not easy, owing to the fact that the writing down of music is incomplete, partly because composers often assume that performers will *know* what they want.

Boult believed that one got better results by being a proper captain who was supposed to know the ship, the water, the charts and what the crew should do. No point in the captain being over-emotional, over-emphatic, rushing about the ship wielding the oilcan or leaping about the rigging.

Boult was a boat man himself. After studying in Germany he conducted in Queen's Hall the first informal run-through of Holst's *The Planets*. Holst was a friend, as was Vaughan Williams; and he had known Elgar even as a schoolboy. Sir Adrian did good work at Birmingham, but his making was also the making of the BBC Symphony Orchestra between 1930-50. Boult was a wonderful trainer and he could give a decent, often an outstanding, performance of practically any type of music. The English School, Brahms, Schubert's *'Great' Symphony in C major*, *Daphnis and Chloe*, *Wozzeck*, *Doktor Faust*, *The Rite of Spring* – he gave great performances of all these.

At the age of sixty he was retired from the BBC, but he immediately took over the London Philharmonic; there were some dispirited years but in his late sixties, seventies and eighties he did great things. What's more, they are on record for all to hear, cherish and learn forgotten traditions by.

Sir Adrian could be very generous but it wasn't always easy to get through to him. He lost his temper about once every fifteen years; he could be sharp if he thought a player inattentive. But he never lost his good manners and his modesty, which is perhaps why his autobiography *My Own Trumpet* is rather unrevealing and disappointing after the first chapter, about his childhood. His strongest term of opprobrium was: 'You silly sausage!' Asked once why his books on conducting concentrate entirely on the practical elements of the craft, never touching on the more intangible, profounder side of the art, he replied: 'Well, yes, there *is* that side of it . . . but I am an Englishman, you know, and I don't go in for that sort of thing very much.'

SIR JOHN BARBIROLLI

B. 1899 LONDON, D. 1970 LONDON

'Love' is the word that comes to mind with Barbirolli, the warmth and love of a man dedicated to music and loving his fellow men and women. Nowadays we tend to think of him for his work with Manchester's Hallé Orchestra and perhaps that *was* his finest achievement. He returned to England in 1943 to remake the Hallé, to lift it up and make it a fine orchestra again, better than it ever had been, perhaps. He could have left it, made more money, more fame elsewhere; but he loved that orchestra and he stayed with it, although in his last years he was often at Houston on a regular basis, and he often 'guested' round the world, achieving wonders (oh, that Mahler *IX* with the Berlin Phil!) on many occasions.

Giovanni Battista Barbirolli was born in Streatham of Italian (Venetian) and French parentage. He was playing concertos on his cello at the age of twelve, became known as a soloist, as a chamber music player, eventually did a bit of conducting with chamber orchestras. Then came opera with the British National Opera Company, Covent Garden, some excellent records accompanying soloists such as Kreisler, Backhaus, Heifetz, Elman; then when he was in charge of the Scottish Orchestra in the mid-Thirties, out of the blue came the call to succeed Toscanini as conductor of the New York Philharmonic. It was almost too much; Toscanini was a hard act to follow. Barbirolli landed some good punches but took some buffetings. However, he survived until three years of England being in the wars became too much for the patriotic Englishman that he was under his Italian skin. In 1949 he was dubbed Sir John.

Barbirolli's repertory was broad, but undoubtedly Puccini, Elgar, Delius, Sibelius, Vaughan Williams, Verdi and Mahler brought out the best in him. Sometimes his love of a tune, phrase, section or passage would lead him to sacrifice the overall shape, but at his best he was incomparable: the power of love triumphed.

BERNARD HAITINK KBE

B. 1929 AMSTERDAM

'Like a handsome Dutch potato,' Sir Peter Hall described him in his *Diaries*. Haitink is said to have laughed about it, which is typical of his modesty. Although if you say to him that he is too modest he replies: 'I'm not modest. If I were, I wouldn't *be* a conductor.' One thing he worries about is being too Dutch, a bit dull. Musicians and audiences don't find him dull, although some might agree that in the past he did not always find enough panache for a Berlioz overture, but that is already long past, Haitink has added brilliance to his more solid qualities: he is one of the few conductors who can conduct really well *all* the classics, romantics *and* this century's works (although not the avant-garde which he doesn't touch). He can accompany and he is good at those operas that he has tackled. He is a man for more seasons than most conductors, satisfying both heart and head.

Most conductors today are private men: their jobs are demanding, what with learning new scores, rehearsing, performing and satisfying the media. You can't make your mistakes in unreported remote lands any more, everything is under the public eye and the big couple of dozen conductors cannot go around with a tiny repertoire anymore. This means time to study, time to think. Haitink is private, despite the interviews, and, now that he is musical director at Covent Garden, the administration.

He can get panicky when things go wrong but almost immediately he can laugh about it. One evening Caballé was the soprano in *Ballo in Maschera* at Covent Garden. Haitink looked up from the pit to give her a cue in the love duet – she wasn't there. He managed to stop the orchestra, then picked up the house phone:

'Get me the stage director,' he hissed to the switchboard girl.

'I can't do that, there's a performance going on,' she said.

'That's where you are entirely wrong,' said Haitink.

He began on the violin, and was encouraged by Leitner to go on conducting courses. His first job was conducting the Netherlands Radio Orchestra, then came a chance with the Concertgebouw whose principal conductor he has been now since 1964; he was with the London Philharmonic from '67-'79, musical director at Glyndebourne from '77 until '87 when he officially took over Covent Garden. We are lucky to have him: he's first-rate and eighteen carat.

LEONID KOGAN

B. 1924 DNEPROPETROVSK, D. 1982 MOSCOW

I n their days, Kogan and David Oistrakh were considered the two foremost Soviet violinists, although in the West, Oistrakh had the edge, being thought sweeter and greater. Kogan's playing was more in line, however, with his younger contemporaries, cooler, perhaps more controlled than his elder colleague.

He gave his first concerts at 17 whilst still a student, playing all over Russia. Like Oistrakh, Kogan won the Brussels competition and then was allowed to make his débuts in Europe, winning acclaim in the USA, South America, Paris and London during the Fifties.

From Bach to Paganini and even to Berg, Kogan gave faultless performances, his cool approach gaining him more favour with the *cognoscenti* than the proletariat. Nevertheless he was the People's Artist and a recipient of the Lenin Prize. Composers liked to entrust their premières to him and even wrote especially for him, amongst them Khrennikov, Karayev, Khachaturian, and Knipper. Kogan also enjoyed playing chamber music, especially in a piano trio with Rostropovich and Gilels (whose sister he married).

LEOPOLD STOKOWSKI

B. 1882 LONDON, D. 1977 NETHER WALLOP

These photographs of Leopold Stokowski were taken during his tenth decade. Records he made at this time – Elgar's *Enigma*, Bizet's *L'Arlésienne* – are so fresh and vigorous they blow you across the room. He was 94 years old, yet the playing has the vitality and the saturated sonority that was typical of Stokowski throughout his life. Put him in front of any orchestra in the world and immediately it would make the Stokowski sound.

Despite everything you've heard to the contrary, Leopold Stokowski was born (and stayed) Leopold Stokowski, in Marylebone, London. His father was a Polish cabinet-maker, his mother an Irishwoman. Young Leopold became a choirboy and, as soon as his feet could reach the pedals, he played the organ. At 13 he entered the Royal College of Music in London; he said he was lucky that none of his teachers tried to persuade him he should learn to walk before he could run. At 18 he was a wildly handsome blond Viking, able to charm birds off trees (and ladies to distraction); he became organist at St James's Piccadilly. After five years an offer came to become organist in a church in New York. He went; already he had his eye on conducting. He still played his favourite Bach but was continually transcribing orchestral works for the organ. Through the social connections of Olga, who became his first wife, he seized the chance to become conductor, at the age of 27, of the Cincinnati Orchestra, despite his inexperience.

Stokowski's hallmark was that he played the orchestra like an organ, using the strings, the woodwind and the brass like three manuals; and it was the undeviating tone of the organ that he sought to bring to the orchestra – this was how the unique Stokowski sound began. His reputation, however, rests on his years with the Philadelphia Orchestra (1912-38) which 'Stokey' built and moulded as an instrument to express his feelings about music. Above all he liked lush string sound. His repertoire was vast: from Bach and the Blue Danube to Schönberg and Charles Ives, via Rachmaninoff and Mahler (including many first performances of their works).

Stokowski was one of the first to see the importance of the gramophone; his own hyped-up orchestration of Bach's organ *Toccata and Fugue in D minor* made history and millions. With that blond hair and his imperious manner, he became 'Mr Music' to the masses, especially after appearing in movies such as *A Hundred Men and a Girl* and Walt Disney's *Fantasia*. He dispensed with his baton and the definite article; he could speak normal English like the Londoner he was, but the blue-rinse ladies were more impressed by a Slavonic accent. The wizard of the podium was a bit of a ham. Oscar Levant once said that if he could have chosen to be present at a great moment in musical history it would have been that instant when Stokowski realised how beautiful his hands were. 'Stokey' had a wry sense of fantasy and humour; he once kidded a would-be biographer that he was born (several years later than in reality) in a forest in Pomerania.

In his search for greater effectiveness Stokowski used to doctor the

scores of the classics. earning the sneers of the purists. Sometimes I think these various tricks were partly the result of boredom: no wonder he got together with Greta Garbo for a much publicized affair. With orchestras he could be ruthless and nasty. needling and sometimes expelling players – his 'You. sir' was the prelude to many a scene. But his magic prevailed: he always knew his scores and his imaginative sense of colour and sound was second to none.

In 1939. after Philadelphia. Stokowski founded the All-American Youth Orchestra. showing his love for young people and his power to build from scratch an orchestra of real quality. From that time on he had several important posts but also went 'guesting' round the world. finally returning to England where he conducted various orchestras and made records. Stokowski believed in the power of music to improve our lives. and he certainly added to that power.

ELIAHU INBAL

B. 1936 JERUSALEM

Inbal studied in his native Jerusalem, then with Celibadache and in Paris and Siena. Winning the Cantelli Competition at the age of 27 opened many doors.

His work has not brought him to the UK very much but he is known to many through his recordings which are legion: the complete original edition of the Bruckner symphonies, all Sibelius, all Scriabin, the four Schumann symphonies. Current projects are a complete Mahler series, Ravel, the major Berlioz works plus nine Beethoven symphonies. He has been musical director of the Frankfurt Radio Symphony since 1974 and he is also principal conductor of La Fenice Opera in Venice, concentrating on Verdi, Mozart and Strauss. He conducted *Figaro* at Glyndebourne.

OLIVER KNUSSEN

B. 1952, GLASGOW

Knussen used to mean Stewart Knussen, red-headed double bass player, one-time chairman of the London Symphony. But he had a son called Oliver and one day when he was 15 this lad conducted his father's symphony orchestra in the Royal Festival Hall. It was an extraordinary sight because the lad was enormous and looked like a badly-stuffed mattress, a bit like a reincarnation of dear old Vaughan Williams. The boy conducted efficiently, the piece wasn't bad, and there were no cries of nepotism hurled towards the basses.

There are family connections over the Pond and Oliver ('Ollie' to one and all) has spent a lot of time over there, attending Tanglewood, the Boston Symphony's summer school, and studying with Gunther Schuller. Ollie knows more about American music than most Brits, but then he knows more about music than most people, full stop. I sometimes wonder if it isn't knowing too much music, going to so many concerts, partly being supportive of his friends, and being sociable, that causes these blocks, these unfinished symphonies, these postponed operas. And now, like Boulez, Ollie has found another way of occupying his time: being an extremely good conductor, much in demand with small orchestras like the London Sinfonietta.

Two operas that finally *did* get finished and put on successfully at Glyndebourne are the one he did with Maurice Sendak's stories and designs – *Where the Wild Things are* – and *Higglety Pigglety Pop!*

Everybody likes Ollie. If he isn't too nice he will probably become one of the most influential musicians in Britain.

CHRISTOPH ESCHENBACH

B. 1940 BRESLAU (NOW WROCLAW, POLAND)

Despite his Polish origins, he is a German pianist who has joined the club – which includes Ashkenazy, Solti, Barenboim and others – of those who now lead baton charges instead of pounding the keys. He stepped up to the podium in 1972 in Hamburg to great critical acclaim for Bruckner's *Symphony no. 3*; engagements followed all over and Eschenbach now spends much less time at the piano. Since 1979 he has been chief conductor in Ludwigshafen, since '81 he has held the same position with the Zurich Tonhalle and he has been on tours to the States and Japan, conducting the Vienna Symphony.

In England critical opinion has usually been adverse, so much so that I was somewhat astonished to receive a sheaf of cuttings full of comments like 'slow movements which threatened to grind to a halt,' 'detrimental extremes of interpretative gesture,' 'a performing tension which has little to do with the music's internal, organic tensions,' and 'a rather pedantic performance of *The Rite of Spring*.' His *Cosi fan tutte* at Covent Garden provoked remarks like, 'Mr Eschenbach's utter unreadiness for such an opera in such a house,' 'the conductor proved at the start so agitated and unsympathetic a director of Mozartian comedy (even breaking his baton in the overture),' 'a bandstand performance of the score.' All these came from critics who had previously – and sometimes in these same notices – commented on or recalled Eschenbach's excellence as a pianist, praising in particular his recordings of the Mozart *Piano Concertos*, directed from the keyboard. But no doubt he will survive even those exceptionally harsh criticisms.

As a pianist, besides Mozart, Christoph has made some fifty recordings of Bartók, Beethoven, Brahms, Chopin, Schubert and Schumann; and many will remember his eloquent rendering of Henze's vast *Piano Concerto No. 2*, with the composer conducting. The work was composed for him, dedicated to him and he gave the première in 1968.

EUGENE ORMANDY

B. 1899 BUDAPEST

Has anyone ever conducted a world-class orchestra for as long as Ormandy directed the Philadelphia? Forty seasons up to 1980, and before that two seasons which he shared with Stokowski, both of them – *and* the public – knowing that he was on trial and that the older Wizard of Sound was about to leave the orchestra he had built up to the point of being *numero uno* as far as sonority, virtuosity and blend were concerned. What a time that must have been! Even thirty years later I couldn't get Ormandy to say a word about those harrowing two years. The amazing thing is that Ormandy did not *disturb* the orchestra; it still went on playing in more or less the same way. Gorgeously. Even now, under Riccardo Muti, the Phily still retains most of the same characteristics, maybe a notch leaner.

Ormandy was born Jenö Blau, he studied violin under Hubay, spent some years as a child prodigy, went to America in 1920 and landed in a cinema orchestra playing accompaniments to the silent movies. After several years in the pits he became conductor of the Minneapolis Orchestra which he raised to a high standard, proof of which can be heard on their magnificent première recordings of the second symphonies of Mahler and Rachmaninoff. Then came the forty gorgeous years with the Phily. . .

PABLO CASALS

B. 1876 CATALONIA, D. 1973 PUERTO RICO

'**M**usic begins with the first note,' he used to say wisely. And who will ever forget the first note of his solo entry on that fabulous recording of the Dvořák *Concerto* that he made in the Thirties, a performance that stands for all time supreme?

With Casals began the modern school of cello playing: Fournier, Tortelier, Rostropovich, Du Pré and Yo Yo Ma are the epigones (most of them have had a fling at the Dvořák, incidentally, but none have surpassed the old Catalan yet).

Casals played his first public notes in the cafes of Barcelona, and was soon dictating them as professor at the Conservatoire. He had his first Paris success in 1899, London (in the Crystal Palace) came in the same year. The USA followed in 1901. From that time on, nothing stopped him until the Spanish Civil War when he went into voluntary exile, vowing never to play in Spain again until Franco was defeated. He kept the vow, although he went as near as he could, founding the Prades Festival in 1950 on the French side of the Pyrenees.

In 1971 Casals conducted his composition *Hymn to the United Nations* (W.H. Auden) at the United Nations in New York. He had settled in Puerto Rico in 1956, founding a festival there and marrying a teenage girl when he was himself 80. On being warned that such a marriage could be fatal, Casals rather characteristically replied: 'I look at it like this: if she dies, she dies.'

Besides playing the cello and composing – mostly for massed cellos – Casals was also a considerable conductor and a member of the most famous piano trio of all times with Alfred Cortot and Jacques Thibaud.

SIR ARTHUR BLISS

B. 1891 LONDON, D. 1975 LONDON

The music of Bliss is underplayed today. At a time when there are champions of Havergal Brian, Frank Bridge, Percy Grainger, George Lloyd and others, it seems strange that Bliss is neglected. His voice is very much his own, especially harmonically, and there is much distinction in his output of lyricism, power and drama. *Checkmate* has survived in the ballet world, *Things to Come* from amongst his film music, *Music for Strings* in the chamber orchestral world and *Morning Heroes*, a choral symphony with a spoken oration, but many other fine works are rarely heard, more's the pity.

Bliss was half American but lived nearly all his life in England; five years in World War I left their mark on him, giving him a rather military bearing, enhancing his natural powers of leadership but scarring him psychologically in a way that he eventually exorcised by writing *Morning Heroes* many years later in 1930.

The beginning of World War II found him teaching in California but he returned in '41 to be Director of Music of the BBC, a fair, generous and able administrator. He was knighted in 1950 and became Master of the Queen's Music in '53.

Bliss's youthful Stravinskian high spirits gave way to his dramatic and lyrical middle period, to be followed in his sixties by a somewhat neo-Elgarian style with too much pomp in it for some of his admirers. But there were flashes of the old fire, notably in the G.M. Hopkins settings for chorus and brass called *The world is charged with the grandeur of God* (1969).

ZUBIN MEHTA

B. 1936 BOMBAY

The Life and Soul of any party he might go to; Mr Can and Does and Will. And the amazing thing about this success story is that Zubin Mehta has made it in a culture far removed from his native Indian one, though his father was founder of the Bombay Symphony Orchestra, a very grand organization even if some rehearsals took place in the Mehta family *living room*.

Zubin learned violin but preferred cricket (he still organizes his London visits to coincide with Test Matches – just as Kubelik does with Wimbledon). At the age of sixteen, however, Zubin stood in for his father at some rehearsals and the willow was exchanged for the baton. Mehta's fellow student at Swarowsky's conducting classes in Vienna was his friend Abbado; unable to get into rehearsals, they joined the Singverein and became choristers under Krips, Kleiber, Karajan and Walter. The first time Zubin heard the Vienna Philharmonic he was so overwhelmed by the beauty of the bottom line that he switched forthwith from violin to double bass. In 1958 he won a conductors' competition in Liverpool, the prize being an (unhappy) year as assistant to the Philharmonic there. Soon he was musical director of Montreal ('61), then Los Angeles ('62 -'77); an affair with the Israel Philharmonic became legalized in '77 and in '78 he took over from Boulez in New York. He frequently 'guests' with the Vienna Philharmonic and at Covent Garden.

Mehta's ebullience is remarkable; he and Daniel Barenboim together are like schoolboys. At the beginning of the Schumann *Concerto*, Zubin will beckon to Danny, then bring the orchestra in on the first chord, leaving Danny to scramble back to the keyboard for the immediate first entry; at the beginning of the slow movement Danny will inveigle Zubin towards the keyboard only to turn the tables on him.

Managements, orchestras, and soloists will all tell you how often Zubin has negotiated difficult situations, cooled down potential blow-outs. He won't suffer unprofessionalism but he is tolerant where others would be egotistic.

'Do you always have this ridiculous seating arrangement?' he asked Covent Garden's orchestral manager.

'Yes, Mr Mehta, would you like to change it?'

'No, better not. *They* won't like it, and there's eighty of them and only one of me.'

DANIEL BARENBOIM

B. 1942 BUENOS AIRES

Word kept on coming through in the Fifties of some kid who played the *Hammerklavier Sonata* and made it sound like the real thing. Most pianists of the older generation looked upon this Beethoven peak as a kind of Everest, only to be attempted after years and years of playing the other 31 sonatas (Schnabel used to go into retreat for several months before his rare performances). Apparently both his mother and father had taught this child to play in Argentina and then the family moved to Israel. So, young Daniel came into the lion's den (hands up the journalist who first thought of that!) and managed to tame *Opus 106* and convince the critics and the public.

He became the darling of the public, played all 32 sonatas and five concertos of L van B, recorded all the Mozart concertos, and played all of Chopin, Schubert, Schumann, and Brahms. He married Jacqueline Du Pre; he became a television star; he played chamber music wonderfully; he went round the world.

There was no music that he didn't know, so it shouldn't have been a surprise when he started conducting, first from the keyboard, then from the podium. Paris took to him in particular and he has been music director of its orchestra since 1975. Opera followed and in Bayreuth in 1986 your scribe was bowled over by the seamless flow and beauty of his conducting of *Tristan*. His Bruckner has the same quality, likewise his Berlioz. With all this, Daniel remains untouched by vanity or the bigtime. He retains his impish sense of humour, his ability to make things work with the minimum of fuss and the maximum of co-operation and friendliness – friendliness to all. His capacity for work is enormous, his abilty to memorize is fabulous. He still plays the piano but cannot always – even with *his* fabulous gifts – compensate for the lack of time spent physically in touch with the keys.

JACQUELINE DU PRÉ

B. 1945 OXFORD

For a brief ten years Jacqueline Du Pré was the golden girl. She first played in public at seven, her adult career began at 16, a year later her performance of the Elgar *Cello Concerto* in the Royal Festival Hall made a deep impression. She was touched by the gods, it seemed, mature beyond her years, surmounting any technical problems her recalcitrant instrument could pose. Her charm, her coltish appearance, her innate musicality quickly made her a name. Her records, her concerts, and her TV appearances soon led to her role as the darling of her public. Jackie became a symbol for the young (the succeeding generation produced a whole batch of outstanding young cellists inspired to emulate her.) She teamed up with the young pianist Daniel Barenboim, married him, made music with him and their friends, Stephen Bishop, Marta Argerich, Radu Lupu, Vladimir Ashkenazy, Pinchas Zuckerman, Zubin Mehta . . .

Jacqueline played with equal success in Europe, Israel and America; the sky was the limit. Generosity was the keyword, she gave everything; she rarely practised, just played, a musician of instinct, nothing was ever quite the same twice.

And then the gods struck down this beauty; they did not kill her but, perhaps worse, they prevented her from doing what she came into the world to do. Her limbs became incapacitated. She gave up playing, eventually had to give up teaching. It is strange how a parallel can be drawn with that other *radiant* music-maker of the post-war years, the singer Kathleen Ferrier. Both had a single ten-year span which enhanced the lives of those who experienced their performances. The records remain . . . and so do the tragedies.

PINCHAS ZUKERMAN

B. 1948 TEL AVIV

Like Perlman, Pinky Zukerman did his studies early, playing everything he could lay his hands on, so that by the age of 13 he knew most of the solo repertoire. Here fate stepped in in the shape of Pablo Casals and Isaac Stern visiting Israel. Stern was so impressed that he got Pinky over to New York, became his legal guardian and arranged for his further musical education. PZ studied with Galamian at Juilliard and played in the students' orchestra there with Perlman and Kyung-Wha Chung sitting in the nearby desks. At the age of 20 Pinky's career was set up for the big time when he stepped in for a sick guardian for a series of concerts throughout America and Europe.

Unlike Perlman, Zukerman began to stray beyond the violin. He has proved himself a remarkable performer on the viola, interesting himself not only in modern music, but also baroque; not only playing, but also conducting. This latter activity began by his leading a chamber orchestra from the violin. Since 1980, Pinky has been music director of the St Paul Chamber Orchestra with which ensemble he has recorded cycles of Mozart, Haydn and Stravinsky, touring extensively in North and South America.

Zukerman is an athlete of a man, a handsome hunk, tremendous fun to meet, with a great sense of humour. Many years ago he met Barenboim and formed a trio with himself and Jacqueline Du Pré as cellist. At that time he also took part in a joyful television film of Schubert's *Trout Quintet* with himself as viola player, Perlman on the top line and Zubin Mehta on the bottom, playing double bass – plus Jackie and Danny. Happy days!

ITZHAK PERLMAN

B. 1945 TEL AVIV

Itzhak Perlman always wanted to play the violin. His father was a barber in Tel Aviv, originally from Poland. When he was four, Itzhak suffered a crippling attack of polio; his parents were sensible about it. Itzhak sits when he plays; audiences sometimes think that he should be spared the indignity of all that walk on for bows, walk off, walk on again, but Itzhak insists on having it that way, so who are we to query it?

When he was 13 Itzhak went to America to appear on the *Ed Sullivan Show*; this was followed by a tour in the States in which several gifted children played at various hotels, hauled out of their 'artists' room' (ie: the kitchen) at midnight to play to the rich. After that experience, says Itzhak, nothing bothers him.

He stayed on in New York, won prizes, worked, débuted, won the prestigious Leventritt Competition. He still lives in New York with his wife Toby and their five children.

Europe and America are the scene of most of his concerts; he is one of the most sought-after of violinists for recordings, TV, concerts. He gives master-classes too. Another form of music-making is his 'crossover' jazz recordings made with André Previn.

RADU LUPU

B. 1945 GALATI

Was this really what Radu Lupu looked like before he grew his beard? Yes, indeed, this was the pianist who won the Leeds Competition in 1969, the dark horse from Romania who had studied in Moscow with the pianist-maker Neuhaus. For the last ten years – or is it more? – he has been like the pard, reminding me of pictures of Rasputin. I don't mean that their characters are similar, only their looks – although there is perhaps something of the mad monk about Radu. Just after Leeds there used to be something slightly dotty about his music-making: a bass line in Beethoven would be suddenly brought to our attention as if he had discovered another *Great Gate of Kiev* under the *Moonlight*. But any trace of the rough peasant has disappeared; in fact I don't think there is another pianist who has quite attained the nobility that Radu achieves in Haydn, Mozart, Schubert and Schumann. Josef Krips once said, 'Beethoven goes to heaven: Mozart *comes* from Heaven.' There is beneath the surface of Mozart some panacea, some perfect state, some secret of life itself that Radu can reveal, and he seems to be able to re-lease that Mozartean quality in the music of other composers. It's a gift of the gods, for sure, backed up by toil and experience.

I remember that at the next Leeds Competition (1972) not abso-lutely everybody immediately saw the quality of Murray Perahia's playing. Radu Lupu canvassed everybody he knew: 'Perahia's *got* to win.' And of course he did. They now record together; their Mozart two-piano *Sonata in D* is as near perfect as you will ever hear.

Radu Lupu was one of that generation – Barenboim, Ashkenazy, Argerich, Bishop, Zukerman, Mehta – that met and made music in London and other places in their twenties and early thirties – kindred spirits of a post-war type of intensely serious artists yet with a lighter side.

EMIL GILELS

B. 1916 ODESSA, D. 1985 MOSCOW

An outstanding pianist. Like Richter, Gilels studied with the pianist-maker Neuhaus. At 22 he won first prize in the prestigious Brussels Competition with the English pianist Moura Lympany, who also won a prize; an early example of Anglo-Soviet friendship occurred when they each played the orchestral part on a second piano for the other. Unfortunately for Gilels and the West, he wasn't allowed 'out' until the Fifties when he made sensational débuts in New York, Paris and London. Gilels was a formidable and sympathetic interpreter of Beethoven; he also won many friends for Prokofiev with his performances of Prokofiev's sonatas and five concertos. Gilels was also a fine Mozart pianist and he loved the music of Grieg, whose entire piano works he recorded. His musician colleagues and indeed all who were lucky enough to have met him, revered and loved Gilels, not least for his sense of humour. He delighted in recounting how, after a recital in mid-West USA, a hick asked him for his autograph after a recital, hung around, chatted until Gilels was ready to go to his hotel, then said: 'Mr Gilels, you've bin so real friendly, ken I jist ask you somethin'? I've heard *both* pronunciations, now which is correct: is it Schu*mann* or Schu*bert* ?'

EMIL GILELS

JASCHA HORENSTEIN

B. 1899 KIEV, D. 1973 LONDON

Fine interpreter of classics, as well as Bruckner, Mahler, Nielsen and the earlier works of composers of the Second Viennese School. He was Russian born, studied with the composer Franz Schreker and the conductor Fritz Busch in Vienna. By the time he was 25 he was working with the Vienna Symphony Orchestra, later conducting in Berlin, then at the Dusseldorf Opera. As with so many of his generation, his life and career were split: being Jewish he could not work in Germany, so he conducted in France, Poland and Belgium, with occasional visits to his homeland. In 1940 he went to America for the first time. Horenstein often worked in the UK, frequently with the BBC, in whose music department he found kindred sprits such as Deryck Cooke, Robert Simpson and Hans Keller. Orchestras recognized in Horenstein a serious-minded musician who was well-equipped to take them deep into the works that he had pondered very considerably. Nor was he without the twinkle that could lighten rehearsals when need be. He made his Covent Garden début with an impressive *Tristan* and he actually died just after a profoundly moving *Parsifal*. Some time previously he had 'died' for a few minutes during a Mahler symphony but had been resuscitated by a doctor who fortunately happened to be seated in the front rows of the concert hall.

ANDRES SEGOVIA

B. 1893 LINARES D. 1987 MADRID

Grand Old Man of the guitar, to him alone we owe the revival of interest in the instrument for playing 'serious' music. Works were especially composed for him by Manuel de Falla, Villa-Lobos, Rodrigo, Ponce, and Castelnuovo-Tedesco. His transcriptions of Bach won him many admirers, and you will find, for example, that a guitarist of a younger generation such as Julian Bream was directly inspired to take up the instrument on hearing not even Segovia in person, but a gramophone record (for Bream it was Tarrega's *Tremolo Study*).

I last heard the Master playing in London at the age – could it be? – of 93 and he could still make magical moments, he still had the traditional Spanish dignity and bearing.

I once asked him about practising, his own and his students'. He said in his strong Spanish accent that he played for 'one hower and one quatter for three times every day.' About the students who boasted that they played for six, seven, eight 'howers' a day, he said scornfully: 'Eef they say that, then I know they are: or donkeys or liars!'

How we were saddened when Segovia died during the final stages of preparing this book.

JULIAN BREAM

B. 1933 LONDON

JOHN WILLIAMS

B. 1941 MELBOURNE

Strange that the Cockney and the Aussie should team up for duets, because their styles are different. John is the perfectionist and although his platform manner is friendly, his playing is many degrees cooler than Julian's. Bream is the communicator par excellence and takes, I would say, more risks than John; Julian doesn't seem to mind a few squeaks here and there, provided he gets the message across. Julian is not above making the odd grimace at the audience whereas John is inscrutable, as befits one who has Chinese blood. Both players cut their teeth on jazz, playing 'electric' as opposed to 'acoustic'. Julian, however, also took up the lute, has his own consort to play 'the ancient stave' from time to time and he has given wonderful recitals with Peter Pears of lute-songs. Even today,

to hear Julian strum a G minor chord on the lute is an experience, let alone a *Lachryma* or two of Dowland.

John 'crosses' right over, he has a superb duo with Cleo Laine and involvement with the group Sky which plays pop and jazz as well as some 'in-between' material.

Having said all that, though, let me knock it all down, because John and Julian seem to blend perfectly when they play duets, somehow welding, melding and osmoseying around in complete accord. Both being such creative, imaginative players seems to urge them on to great feats of daring and ensemble, not so much 'anything you can do I can do better' but 'oh, you're doing it that way, here, let me have a bash too.'

SVIATOSLAV RICHTER

B. 1915 ZHITOMIR, UKRAINE

Not mean but certainly a moody and magnificent pianist. Take his first three Royal Festival Hall recitals in London, for example. We had heard about this mystery man for years; a few of us had listened to some scratchy Soviet records and his qualities shone through. But the recitals were very mixed: some wonderful Prokofiev but then a Schubert *B flat Sonata* where his slow tempi seemed not at all geared to the acoustic of the hall. He seemed to be playing to himself, not trying to project to us; people felt excluded and they coughed. It was the same with the Chopin *Polonaise-Fantaisie* until he suddenly came to life with those amazing double and treble trills towards the end. Richter won't make concessions; he is susceptible to atmosphere; he will switch on and off. Take as another example his two recordings of Prokofiev's *Fifth Concerto*: the one with the Polish conductor Rowicki is alive, it vibrates with meaning and sensibility; the other, with Maazel, is lifeless and meaningless, tempi totally different. Both are technically excellent, mind you. Richter cannot bungle anything; his technique is second to none.

Anthony Phillips told me how he once 'nannied' Richter around America on a tour, interpreting for the pianist, who speaks no English, and acting as his driver. This was some time ago and was Richter's first encounter with a car whose roof could be opened at the flick of a switch. Richter's response to an incredible sight was the same as the crowd's response to a good pass in the bullring: he would throw his hat in the ring or . . . into the Niagara Falls or the Grand Canyon. The bigger the wonder, the more hats got thrown away. Richter disliked American cultures and habits – their cocktails in particular – so every night yet another horrific concoction would be ordered and very carefully analysed in a little notebook kept handy for the purpose.

The Liszt *Sonata* was played many times on the tour; in each

performance there were many different features: speed, tempo and mood. He is a strange man, liable to get a sudden obsession, such as, for instance, for a certain kind of Japanese piano that nobody else could enthuse about. Nowadays he has decided that his records made at public concerts are better than studio ones; I think he is right.

He responds marvellously to artists he likes and admires: the Brahms songs with Fischer-Dieskau, the sonatas with Rostropovich, or the one-piano-four-hands recitals with Benjamin Britten in Aldeburgh. These and his best solo recitals or concertos are on a different plane from ordinary concert happenings. Meeting him is also a life-enhancing experience; he talks to you – *at* you – as if you are the only person in the world, certainly the only person in the world that he wants to talk to.

HANS SCHMIDT-ISSERSTEDT

B. 1900 BERLIN, D. 1973 HAMBURG

'**D**oktor Hans' was a fine, no-nonsense conductor who never let you down, and never let the composer down. For over a quarter of a century he was in charge of the orchestra that he founded in 1945, the Radio Symphony Orchestra of Hamburg, known in the early days as the NWDR (North West German Radio). In 1951 Dr Hans and his orchestra were the first foreign ensemble to play in the re-built Free Trade Hall in Manchester. In London they were to give us not only superb and classical performances of Beethoven and Brahms but to show us, for the first time, how the music of Michael Tippett should sound on the orchestra: their performance of his *Concerto for double string orchestra* was a revelation. Some time later, HSI did the same for Tippett's oratorio *A Child of our Time*.

He was principal conductor of the Stockholm Philharmonic from 1955-64, and was at Glyndebourne in 1958 for *Figaro*, and at Covent Garden in 1962 for *Tristan*. He was frequently in the UK as a guest conductor and a fine memorial to him is his recorded Beethoven cycle with the Vienna Philharmonic. Was it a touch of reserve, a lack of ambition or the last ounce of energy that prevented his becoming a household name?

'Honour your German masters,' sings Hans Sachs, but a few centuries later he might have added, 'Honour the German system of music-making.' To every town worthy of the name its own symphony orchestra and its own opera house — over sixty in West Germany. This training ground has bred many of the conductors whose faces we see in this book. The young men start by being repetiteurs, coaching the singers, cueing the performers from the prompter's box, conducting the off-stage bands and the chorus, giving the signals for the curtains. Then they are given an operetta and maybe an opera to conduct at the end of a run or when someone falls ill. They keep at it, become assistant conductor at another town maybe, finally making it to the level of music director and are at last given a chance to conduct one of the dozen symphony concerts that the hard-working opera orchestra gives during the winter months.

This is how Eugen Jochum worked his way up, by hard work, patience, luck and, of course, great talent. A coach at Munich at the age of 22, then at Kiel, he later became assistant conductor there. He was chief conductor at Duisberg, then at Berlin Radio and the State Opera. in '34 he was to be seen in Hamburg with the State Opera, and with the Philharmonic in the same town from '34 to '49. It was in Hamburg that he somehow managed to conduct composers such as Hindemith and Mendelssohn years later than anywhere else in Nazi Germany.

In '49 Jochum moved south again, to direct the Bavarian Radio Symphony Orchestra for a dozen years, then for three years he shared the Concertgebouw Orchestra in Amsterdam with Haitink, after which he was chief conductor at Bamberg until '78. For the past thirty years Jochum has visited England regularly, an honoured guest with the London Philharmonic and with the London Symphony, becoming in '75 the latter orchestra's conductor laureate.

ISAAC STERN

B. 1920 KREMENETS/KRIMINIESZ

'Leave no tone un-Sterned' was the snap advice given to a student asking for guidance from Yehudi Menuhin – although the advice was given by Lady Menuhin before the master himself had time to take breath. It's good advice too: every tone Stern makes has been thought about, felt deeply and executed with sureness. There is a terrific warmth about him, both in the playing and in the way he has lived his life, the way he has helped individuals and institutions. Stern saved the Carnegie Hall from demolition; and who can ever forget the way Stern taught those youngsters in the film *To China – with Love ?*

His family left the town on the Polish/Russian border (hence the two versions of his birthplace given above) when young 'Ike' was a few months old. In San Francisco he switched from piano to violin when he was eight; after his New York recital début at 17 he had no more lessons. Stern learned much, he has said, from playing chamber music: first as a young boy playing with local musicians, later at Prades with Casals and the first-rate team with which the old cellist surrounded himself. Stern means 'star' in German and Isaac soon became one; listen to his Mozart or the Brahms concertos, the *D major* Prokofiev or the Stravinsky with the composer conducting.

Stern is rounded as to personality and shape. I am sorry that Laelia caught him on a day when he wasn't wearing his spectacles pushed up to his receding hairline. His speaking voice is measured, ingratiating and not used parsimoniously. In a radio interview I asked my first question and got 25 minutes' first-rate stuff; he rang up next day to apologize for not giving me enough time for a second question. Some American musicians have been known to mutter veiled accusations about Ike heading the musical Mafia over there. Sure, he likes power, but I think he uses it benevolently. You cannot distrust Ike – or dislike him – or deny his sovereignty as a violinist.

KARLHEINZ STOCKHAUSEN

B. 1928 NR. COLOGNE

Like so many avant-gardists, if you meet him, you find that Karlheinz Stockhausen can be perfectly charming. His speaking voice is well-modulated and ingratiating; he has the same riveting presence that Wagner must have had. Actually, looking at Laelia Goehr's photograph reminds me of the well-known daguerrotype of Chopin in his last years.

In his three-score years Karlheinz has been through most of the avant-garde hoops: first of all using *musique concrète* and tapes to create his early *Gesang der Jünglinge* in which he made a magical mix with a boy's voice; he then took Webern's theories to logical (?) extremes, serialising not only notes but also octave pitch, intensity, dynamics and so on. Another phase was the aleatoric or chance method, quasi-improvising with given material; taken to its extremity, this produced *Aus den sieben Tagen* (1968), in which the players were asked to listen carefully and play 'in the spirit of the universe' (Stockhausen failed to take the British sense of humour into account; this piece proved not to travel well). He then tried the space game with orchestras or loudspeakers dotted round the hall; another phase involved using one chord for 75 minutes, sometimes with mesmerizing effects; then there was the medley of national anthems (I'll get shot if I recall that Malcolm Arnold has composed his own versions of two of these games, far shorter and more effectively); there was even one work that was in D minor.

During the last decade, Stockhausen has been working on a vast set of operas, one for each day of the week. It was once put to a musician who had worked with him a lot that Stockhausen seemed to think he was God. His reply: 'Jesus Christ minimum.'

VICTORIA POSTNIKOVA

B. 1944 MOSCOW

Seldom has a second prize winner created such a furore as Victoria did at the Leeds Competition in 1966. There were argie-bargies on the jury, resignations were threatened and Victoria did well out of it because Hans Keller and Sir William Glock from the BBC were on that jury. She not only played as though made of fire and ice combined but she also looked stunning, like some pre-Soviet fairy-tale princess. Victoria has continued to do well for herself, although she has not made *quite* such a big career for herself as was predicted for her at the time. But her playing of Tchaikovsky, Rachmaninoff, Prokofiev, and Shostakovich is inspiring. Nowadays she is often to be heard accompanied from the podium by her husband, Gennadi Rozhdestvensky. They also play piano duets extremely well and, where possible, they take with them Victoria's son from her first marriage.

GENNADI ROZHDESTVENSKY

B. 1931 MOSCOW

On the podium Gennadi looks like a Soviet general. very much in charge. economic with his gestures but imperiously flicking a finger towards a wind-player for an entry. an outstretched arm towards a percussionist. a curled. inviting left hand to the strings.

He is economic with rehearsals too. a habit which at first delighted the BBC Symphony Orchestra when he became their chief conductor in 1978. but dismayed them as time went on. Players like to play through difficult passages several times. singers like to have piano rehearsals; Gennadi was very reluctant to give them. It is true that he

He is a marvellous accompanist: hear him especially when his wife, the adorable Victoria Postnikova, plays Rachmaninoff or Prokofiev: the result is superb. But rather often the feeling is that the surface of the music is brilliantly delineated but that the performance rarely goes deeper. Whether extra rehearsals would make any difference is questionable.

Rozhdestvensky loves to conduct Mozart, but that composer is too revealing. In private Gennadi is delightful, a friendly egghead on a round but springing body. It is a wonder for some that he and Victoria have remained within the Soviet Union, but then they travel in the West such a lot that perhaps they consider that they have the best of both worlds. Gennadi is a good pianist and gives fine performances, four hands at one piano, with Victoria.

SIR GEORG SOLTI

B. 1912 BUDAPEST

'Conducting is a mysterium consisting of the mixing together of some sort of spiritual, inspirational and interpretational guidance with mental control, which is something you can never leave out. The right mixture is like an alchemist's secret. Too much control and you lose intensity; too little control, and you become too rhapsodic and abandoned. It's always a question of this mixture of emotion and control, and every conductor must have it.'

Thus spake Sir Georg (in an interview with Helen Matheopoulos). Yet consider . . . in his youth two of the greatest conductors were Toscanini and Furtwängler. The Italian veered towards too much control but rarely lost intensity; the German veered towards the rhapsodic but rarely lost control. Yet Toscanini sometimes seemed to be drilling his men and Furtwängler relied on great understanding from his. Solti is a rare case of a conductor who started off in the Toscanini mould – all energy, fire and discipline – but now seems to be veering towards the Furtwänglerian style, more relaxed and with a greater amount of improvisation.

Although from an early age he wanted to be a conductor, Solti was kept from orchestras by a Swiss wartime isolation, keeping in touch with performances by playing the piano – evidence of which exists in the form of several fine 78's with the excellent German violinist Georg Kulenkampf. As soon as the war was over the opera called to him: Munich 1946-52, Frankfurt 1952-61, Covent Garden 1961-71. The London decade was a time of outstanding though not continuous success: some wonderful Strauss, a *Ring* and a sensational *Moses and Aaron* by Schönberg produced by Sir Peter Hall were the highest lights. Perhaps the English way of life and sense of humour had a good effect on the volatile Hungarian. He became a British subject, was knighted by the Queen, refused a further term at Covent Garden and took on the musical direction and conducting of the Chicago Symphony. One of the world's finest orchestras, and one of its finest conductors took to each other and the partnership is a supreme one still.

ERICH LEINSDORF

B. 1912 VIENNA

By the age of 22, Erich Leinsdorf was thought good enough to be engaged as assistant conductor to Bruno Walter and Toscanini at the Salzburg Festival. For the next three years he was also thought good enough to be re-engaged. With the help of the older conductors he was taken on as an assistant conductor at the Metropolitan Opera in New York. Leinsdorf was soon in charge of the German repertoire until 1943, returning there from 1957 to '62. In between he had stints with the Cleveland and Rochester Orchestras and the New York City Opera. His finest hour was his eight years with the Boston Symphony Orchestra as successor to Charles Munch. After this, the world was open to Leinsdorf and he guest-conducted in most corners of the globe and in many of its centres. He had a wonderful command of the orchestra, an infallible ear and a wide knowledge of repertoire.

Erich is a stimulating companion with a mind well-stocked with many more subjects than music. I never met a man with a hairier chest or back (but don't ask me how I know: the answer is so dull).

MSTISLAV ROSTROPOVICH

B. 1927 BAKU, USSR

Artist, musician, cellist, pianist, conductor, man. Put the words in any order and then put an exclamation mark after each; so far that's !!!!!! What a power-house of energy! What a fountain of love!

On his first visit to the Aldeburgh Festival I came across him standing by a grassy path on which people were crossing from the car park to Orford Church. 'Slava' (as everybody calls him) wasn't waiting for anybody, he wasn't playing at that particular concert, he was just standing there, beaming rather shyly at every person that came by. We all knew who he was; he didn't know any of us. It was just a gesture of friendliness towards us all. It's the only time I have seen shyness on that face.

At one of those early Aldeburgh concerts he played with Benjamin Britten Debussy's *Cello Sonata* which the composer once said was about Pierrot. And there is something of that moonstruck clown about Slava's infinitely variable, comic, irresistible, vulnerable and sometimes vulnerous face. That squidgy nose, that elongated mouth, that amazing jaw – it is like several faces amalgamated into one. Its owner would *have* to be some kind of clown or some kind of musical genius. Slava is larger than life and everything he does is larger than life.

Some of us think that this all adds up to a better cellist and pianist than (*so far*, I hasten to add) conductor. It is fantastic to see how he has pulled up that Washington orchestra to be an instrument of excellent quality. But the poor things are made to play within an inch of their lives every moment of the day, the evening, the concert. Too much voltage. The best I have heard him do was with the student orchestra and the student opera at Aldeburgh.

Slava's piano playing for his wife Galina Vishnevskaya for her performances of Russian songs is of a rare quality, akin to Britten

playing for Pears or Richter for Fischer-Dieskau. Even then, Slava's irresistible humour can sometimes come to the fore: himself carrying on the piano part for a performance of Mussorgsky's *Songs and Dances of Death*, the said score upon being placed on the music desk of the piano upside-down proved to be a vocal score of *Trovatore* which the bewildered page-turner was violently nudged into turning over every minute or so.

His courage in standing up to the Soviet regime was as great as his sorrow when he and Galina were stripped of their citizenship some years later. Their hearts are still mainly in Russia despite their success elsewhere, with their houses and apartments in Paris, London, Aldeburgh, Washington and 'up-state New York'. On his 60th birthday Rostropovich was made a K.B.E. by the Queen.

His music-making is rare in that he can give so much in feeling and emotion without losing control: let us hope that he is preserved for years to come. He lives dangerously, he takes risks: with politics, with his baton, with his cello, with his health. But a Slava who took care wouldn't be Slava.

THE MANCHESTER SCHOOL

They were all born in the 1930s and were fellow composition students of a remarkable teacher and composer called Richard Hall at the Royal Manchester School of Music. *Alexander Goehr* had been born in Berlin but the other three – *Harrison Birtwistle*, *Peter Maxwell Davies* and *John Ogdon* – were from the North of England. Formidable brains all four: Ogdon became best known as a pianist; he won the coveted Tchaikovsky Prize in Moscow in 1962. In the early days he played his own compositions and those of the other three, notably a wild, not to say improbable, *sonata* for trumpet and piano by Peter Maxwell Davies (played with another member of the School, Elgar Howarth, now better known as a conductor).

Davies, Birtwistle and Goehr made their living at various times by teaching: Davies early in his career at Cirencester School For Boys, Birtwistle at Cranborne Chase early on too, Goehr since 1976 as Professor of Music at Cambridge after an earlier period as BBC music administrator. Birtwistle has been music director at the National Theatre in London whilst Davies was for ten years director of the Orkney Festival and the Dartington Summer School of Music. Thus, in one way or another, all four composers have had a big influence on the musical life of the UK.

≡ SIR PETER MAXWELL DAVIES

B.1934 SALFORD

Ruthless People was the film he was going to see when I last met him and he is showing that side of himself here to the camera. Any first-rate creative talent needs to have ambition, determination and steel elbows; Max has them, plus a lightning quick brain, a retentive memory, a talent for organizing, a capacity for charming people, controlling situations and commanding others, especially young people. He is anti-sentimental but has 'nostalgia' for the Middle Ages and the 1920s; thus his music can switch from austerity and the recondite medieval musical devices to 'camp' such as foxtrots that even include the sound of a gramophone record running down. His theatre pieces range from the wild expressionism of *Revelation and Fall* (complete with loudhailer) through the crazed Handelianism of *Eight Songs for a Mad King* down to the simple tunefulness of his *Cinderella* children's opera. Like Britten, Davies has written many works for social occasions, and for friends and groups, such as his own Fires of London (extinguished in 1987 after 20 busy, successful years round Europe).

Since 1970 he has been turning increasingly from the smaller combos to opera – *Taverner*, a big piece with some big music in it – as well as to ballet – a full-long *Salome* – and three *Symphonies*. For many years PMD has lived intermittently on the remote Orcadian island of Hoy where he can enjoy solitude and his capacity for incredible amounts of hard work. At the latest count, there are some 140 works to his credit, a formidable amount when you consider the time he spends in performing, directing, organizing, teaching and travelling. He can be good fun too.

JOHN OGDON

B. 1937 MANSFIELD

He comes on to the platform looking like some shambling, overweight bear, blinking a little at the light. Within the first minute or so he will have played so many notes so quickly that you forget the bear, then when the notes get slower you realize the extreme beauty of sound he is getting. At the end, sweating profusely, he will shake everybody's hand in sight, always sharing the applause with the conductor and the orchestra, diving into the body of the players to shake hands with anyone who has had a prominent solo.

I first met John years ago, took him to lunch to discuss what he was going to play at two concerts at Dartington. We discussed items: 'I believe you play one or two of *The Art of the Fugue* ?'

'Yes, but I could play it all if you like,' he replied.

'And you play the second Hindemith *Sonata* ?'

'Yes, but I could learn the other two if you want.'

Of course he does memorize at the speed of light, but even so . . .

He was asked to give master-classes – not by me, who had seen his extreme shyness – but his voice didn't carry more than three feet and his sentences petered out after three words. But sessions in private revealed his needle-sharp perception, and his analytical sense, countered somewhat by his reluctance to say anything that might ruffle the students' confidence.

His own playing can be baffling. I have known him ignore most of the composer's directions on occasions and yet produce a more penetrating insight into the piece than an accurate one. I find him at his best in music that really gives him something to get his teeth into but that also engages his brain cells: Busoni, Szymanowski, late Beethoven, Prokofiev, even . . . Ogdon.

ALEXANDER GOEHR

B. 1932 BERLIN

The young Sandy told one of his colleagues that his ambition was to be professor of music at Oxford or Cambridge. It took him some twenty years to achieve this, via the BBC, being associate prof. in Yale, then full professor at Leeds from '71 to '76.

After leaving Manchester he went to Paris, studying with both Olivier Messiaen and Yvonne Loriod. The first work of his to come before a wider public, partly because it was recorded on the back of a work of Tippett's, was his *Little Symphony* (though it was not particularly little in duration) of 1963, written in memory of his father, Walter, the conductor, who had done a great deal to propagate the music of Tippett.

Other landmarks in Goehr's composing career include the big choral cantata *Sutter's Gold*, several pieces given at the Brighton Festival by his champions Jacqueline Du Pré and Daniel Barenboim, and his fascinating opera *Arden muss sterben* (titled *Arden Must Die* when eventually given in the UK, long overdue). Sandy has great charm, a sense of humour, a way with words and a powerful mind (the Reith lectures that he gives in 1987 will be humane and politically instructive, no doubt).

HARRISON BIRTWISTLE

B. 1934 ACCRINGTON

None too forthcoming is our Harry. He comes from up North, where they're a bit suspicious of folks. Once he knows you, it might be alright; or then again, it might not. If you like his music, then he'll thaw. And increasing numbers of people do like his music, even though he hasn't written an ingratiating bar in his life. So his life has been hard work because composing doesn't come quickly (unlike with some you could mention). Not that he would want it to. He has been helped though by a publisher who took him on at a reasonably early age. Michael Kennedy once wrote that Birtwistle's 'music is marked by genuine lyrical impulse built on dramatic use of *ostinato* [recurring material] and repeated thematic fragments. A strong poetic feeling pervades all his work.'

There is something raw and ritualistic about Harry's music, it cuts through the bone. If you don't know it, start perhaps with *Tragoedia*, or *Medusa*, or *Cantata*, all chamber works; or the orchestral *Triumph of Time*; then the operas *Down by the Greenwood Side*, *Yan Tan Tethera* or the mammoth *Orpheus*.

Once, many years ago, Alexander Goehr said to Peter Maxwell Davies: 'Wouldn't it be strange if Harry turned out to be the best composer of us?'

HANS WERNER HENZE

B. 1926 GUTERSLOH

The Prince Charming of modern music. Henze's is contemporary music without tears – not all the time; on occasions he can put the boot in. But at his best, his music is positively sybaritic, richly textured with celesta, guitar, harps or mandolines lulling the ear. Then the next piece will remember that its composer has loyalties to Cuba if not Russia, get out the brass and the red flag, don't forget the workers, perhaps one of them would like a glass of champagne. But even in the middle of a fairly nasty piece like *We Come to the River* (the opera, words by Edward Bond, performed at Covent Garden in 1976), there is some fine, sumptuous music, likewise in the W.H. Auden-texted *Elegy for Young Lovers*, given its British première at Glyndebourne in 1962.

'My dear, I think I've starting writing some good music at last,' Hans will say disarmingly. But the mixture still seems pretty much the same after composing at least half-a-dozen of everything – operas, ballets, symphonies, string quartets, cantatas, film scores, theatre pieces, concertos. You name it: Henze has written it. Try the *Oboe and Harp Concerto* he wrote for the Holligers or the full orchestral *Barcarola* that begins like Britten's *Sinfonia da Requiem*, ends with the *Tristan* act III prelude chord, takes in the *Eton Boating Song*, picks up Styx and has some good Henze in between. Hans had a tiff with the Homeland, a long love affair with Italy, made it up with Germany, loves the good life, but must surely spend the majority of his time writing these endless scores which people lap up.

LEONARD BERNSTEIN

B. 1918 NR. BOSTON

Who has done the most for music since the time of World War II? Karajan, who has made more records than anyone else? Britten, or Shostakovich, who have written the best music, and got through to the most people? Or Bernstein? Maybe . . .

As a conductor he compares favourably with the best: like Karajan, Bernstein does some awful things, too sentimental, over the top, but at his best in Beethoven, Schumann, Mahler, Strauss, Debussy, Nielsen, Shostakovich, and most American music, he is supreme. There are not many records of him playing *and* conducting but those that exist are again very, very good. As a composer of 'serious' music he has written one or two good pieces – the *Serenade* (really a concerto for violin), the *Chichester Psalms*. As a composer of musicals he is in a class of his own – think of *West Side Story*, *On the Town*, *Wonderful Town* and the neglected *Candide*, brilliant and lasting ! Then there is Bernstein the educator, the TV lecturer whose illustrated talks have brought music to millions.

And of course it is the millions that we have to take into consideration if we ask subjective questions such as who has done the most for music. Because of his exposure through records, radio, TV, personal appearances in concert or in the opera house, teaching at Tanglewood . . . yes, I think we would have to say not 'Bernstein, maybe' but 'Bernstein, *yes*.'

If art is a form of love, then Bernstein is a great artist and a great lover. He loves people (to death sometimes!) and he wants to share music with people. What does it matter that he has spread his talents? How do we know that, say, his symphonies would be any better if he didn't spend so much time conducting?

Something that the camera does not tell you about Lennie unless it captures him walking *through* the orchestra is how small he is. That shows how well proportioned he is. He rarely stops talking, why should he? He is so good at it. But he is also a listener, he really does like people individually as well as in the abstract; besides, listening gives him a chance to smoke (he is such a smoker that there is even a Bernstein employee whose job is to hand him a lighted cigarette so that he can take a puff between bows. Crazy? What about Karajan then who has an employee whose job is to hand the maestro a brush and comb between bows?) Adlai Stevenson once said 'Success is all very well as long as you don't inhale.' Lennie inhales, he likes applause, it is what makes him tick, what makes him, and what will make him, until his Last Post, a Wunderkind. He has his hang-ups, his guilt complexes, and like anyone who is successful at some things but not at others, I am sure that it is his desire to succeed in serious music that gnaws him most, that makes him alternately love and hate to look at a sheet of blank manuscript paper.

HENRYK SZERYNG

B. 1918 WARSAW

A most accomplished violinist – brilliant, elegant, suave – he plays all the notes and studied composition long enough to know what lies beneath the notes. Nevertheless he is not what you'd call an intellectual player. With certain composers, this is fine: with Paganini, with Chausson's *Poème*, with Ravel's *Tzigane*, with his fellow countryman Szymanowski's ecstatically beautiful *Concerto No.1*; but with Bach, Beethoven and Brahms you begin to wish that, possessed as he is of everything a violinist could want in the way of technique, Henryk would use it as a springboard to make *really* satisfying music. His playing is in tune but not with the infinite (alas! not my phrase, but Virgil Thomson's).

Henryk is a thoroughly nice fellow, if you can get beyond the pomp and circumstance. If only he had more humour and could laugh at his natty dressing, his la-di-da voice, the outbreaks of me-myself-and-I that he doesn't really need. The old ladies love him because he remembers everybody's name in the artists' room, the names of their relatives, even their poodles; and he isn't just putting it on – he really cares for people. Get him away by himself and he is a good friend, entertaining companion, with a generous, well-stocked head.

PAUL TORTELIER

B. 1914 PARIS

Paul Tortelier or Don Quichotte? Once upon a time there was a TV performance of Richard Strauss's tone-poem in which the solo part was played by our hero. Superimposed on the image of him playing his cello was one of the famous Gustave Doré illustrations of the quixotic knight. And there is something of the naive Don about Paul: his ideas of changing the world are . . . well, quixotic, despite his patent sincerity.

Paul nurtures two ambitions: one is to change the world; the other is to be recognized as a great composer. Some of his little bits and pieces are charming, especially those for cello ensembles, but his *Israel Symphony* (1956), composed during a year living in a kibbutz, has not come many people's way yet.

Tortelier's first recognition as a cellist came at a competition when he played the Elgar *Concerto* (which he plays wonderfully) in France, but this only led to orchestral positions: Monte Carlo '35-'37, Boston '37-'40, Paris '46-'47. His solo breakthrough came with *Don Quixote* in London with Beecham.

England has continued to love Tortelier, to love him for his playing, for his charisma, and also for being every Englishman's idea of a Frenchman; he has a strong accent that seems to be daily watered to keep its freshness and that touch of oh-so-Continental temperament. Adorable man and, you would think, quite impossible to live with; and yet there is his wife Maud, also a very good cellist, also adorable. Then there are the children: Yan Pascal metamorphosing from a violinist to a conductor; and Maria de la Pau, an excellent pianist. They play as a trio, the two cellists as a duo; maybe Don Quixote himself could have become a family man.

LORIN MAAZEL

B. 1930 NEUILLY

Conducting, Lorin Maazel explained to the *New York Times* a few years ago, is an art which requires long training, long maturing and constant re-working (he was having a swipe at world-famous virtuosi instrumentalists edging into the conducting profession). Only maturity can give access to the true flow of a work and a sense of the time that evolves from its first note to its last. Only three conductors, continued Maazel, had the ability (in 1978) to maintain the necessary standards of the art of conducting: Herbert von Karajan, Georg Solti and Lorin Maazel.

Maazel was born in France but studied in America, a child prodigy violinist, later a young conductor of leading American orchestras. Stepping down the line at 18, he became a violinist in the Pittsburgh Orchestra; stepping up again, he started conducting opera in Italy, made Bayreuth at 29, and Salzburg three years later. The

world was and is his oyster. He chose Berlin for six years, directing the Radio Orchestra there and the Deutsche Oper; there were débuts at La Scala, Milan and at the Vienna Opera; he became assistant principal conductor of the New Philharmonia, London, '70-'72, and music director of the Cleveland from '72 to '82.

There is nothing that Maazel cannot conduct well, but it is difficult to know why some performances work, some don't. Technically he is superb; he knows everything there is to be known . . . except about human nature, especially his own. Sometimes he acts as if he were not human and then he finds out the hard way. He rubs the players up the wrong way; occasionally he has come to a full stop in the middle of an operatic performance and the curtain has had to be brought down. But most of the time he is eminently worthy to be included in the list of names he mentioned (did he *forget* Bernstein?) Despite his coldness as a person, there is warmth in the performances: Verdi's *Requiem*, *Porgy and Bess*, Mahler, Prokofiev – exemplary!

It was typical of Maazel that he thought he could be director of the Vienna Opera and make it work, typical of Vienna that they forced him out, and typical of Vienna that they should start to cheer his performances again after he had resigned.

RUDOLF KEMPE

B. 1910 DRESDEN, D. 1976 ZURICH

Kempe studied conducting in his home town with Fritz Busch but started his professional life as an oboeist, taking a principal's job in the Leipzig Gewandhaus Orchestra from 1929 to '36. His conducting début was also in Leipzig with Lortzing's *Der Wildschütz*. A series of opera jobs after the war in East Germany, Chemnitz, Weimar and Dresden, landed him in the West for three years at Munich; in the middle years he made his Covent Garden début in '53, and conducted the *Ring* cycles in London. Concerts with

the Royal Philharmonic Orchestra saw him appointed their principal conductor in '63; in 1970 they made him their artistic director for life, not knowing how short a time that was to be. Kempe also conducted at the Met in New York, at Zurich with the Tonhalle, in Munich again, and he had just begun as principal conductor with the BBC Symphony when he died.

He was not a showy conductor but he was a truly great one. Kempe followed Richard Strauss's maxim that the orchestra should sweat but not the conductor. He was not an intellectual. He worked hard at his scores, his technique was faultless, his ego minimal — it was almost impossible to get him to talk about conducting. He just did it and lived the music with all that was apparent in it and all that was beneath the surface. Kempe lived Furtwängler's saying that the conductor's task was 'the sensualization of the spiritual and the spiritualization of the sensual.'

In Laelia's picture you can see how deepset were his eyes, eyes that kept a shy man private. But just once a year he would conduct a concert in which he showed two more facets of himself: first his ability to conduct light music — waltzes that really made you want to get up and dance; he also indulged in genuinely funny behaviour, very underplayed stuff that showed you what an excellent actor he could be. Kempe could have done anything he set his mind to. Alas, during his last illness, he showed no will to live.

From Haydn to Richard Strauss, Kempe was peerless, not excluding unexpected composers like Puccini and Delius, a festival of whose music he conducted in 1962. Three months before the Delius concerts in Bradford, I asked Kempe what his view of Delius was. He hummed and hawed, and finally said that he didn't have one yet. When would he have one? When he opened the scores, he said, exploding with laughter.

ANDOR FOLDES

B. 1913 BUDAPEST

Not unlike a china effigy of a tubby mandarin, Andor's voice is about an octave higher than you would expect. When I last visited him he was living at Rupperswil, a pretty suburb on the lake near Zurich. He showed me his wonderful collection of miniature sculptures, all modern: Arp, Giacometti, Armitage, and Henry Moore maquettes. We talked of Bartók and how, in the early days, those students who dared to play it took very seriously the fact that his best known piece then was called *Allegro Barbaro*. Foldes played it and other pieces of his to Bartók, who kept on saying: 'Don't play it so Bartókish.' He said that Bartók's playing was remarkable for being just the opposite of *barbaro*, a singing *legato*. He turned pages for Bartók when he and his wife played the Schubert *F minor Fantasia*. Bartók would not teach composition so Foldes studied with Dohnanyi and he later published some piano pieces, as well as books on piano technique. Andor won the International Liszt Prize in Budapest in 1933. In '39 he emigrated to the USA and became an American citizen. After the war he played all over the world, specializing in the works of Bartók.

PIERRE FOURNIER

B. 1906 PARIS, D. 1986 PARIS

An elegant, distinguished looking, very French man with a face whose lines suggested that he had suffered during his life. As regards his career, there seem to have been no problems. The pain in his life was caused by the polio that attacked him as a child and left him with a bad limp – he always used a stick when walking.

At the age of nine Fournier took up the cello. Success came to him quite early as a soloist, he always delighted in playing chamber music and he was also a fine teacher. Fournier played in the first, private, performance of Fauré's late *String Quartet*. That was in 1925 and he continued to play contemporary music as well as classical and romantic works. Frank Martin and Martinu composed concertos for him, Poulenc a sonata. When Casals would no longer play in the trio with Thibaud and Cortot, Fournier took his place. In 1947 he joined Szigeti, Primrose and Schnabel for trios and quartets in many capitals of Europe and at the Edinburgh Festival. I can remember one performance in the Central Hall, London, where the violinist broke a string and Fournier shocked Schnabel by tappping him gently on the shoulder, the pianist having continued playing, unaware of the interruption in the music. Later on Fournier joined Szeryng and Kempff in piano trios.

Despite his air of being the *grand seigneur*, Fournier joined in easily with pupils and colleagues in the lighter side of professional life. At one time he was married to Leda, former wife of Piatigorsky; latterly he lived in Geneva with a Japanese wife.

OLIVIER MESSIAEN

B. 1908 AVIGNON

What does the expression in Messiaen's face reveal? A man dazzled by the glory of God and who has spent most of his life trying to share that devotion with others through his compositions? Or a man whose eyesight has been impaired by the constant reading and writing of music? Both, perhaps, and with cause. He has also used his sight to strain after the flight of birds because Messiaen has been a keen ornithologist all his life. He delights in their colours and aerial movements, and has systematically recorded their songs not only for private research but for his music. Hundreds of bird calls are to be found both in works as specifically named as *Oiseaux exotiques* for piano and orchestra, and the vast solo piano *Catalogue des oiseaux* and also in many other works, the majority of which have religious titles like *Trois petites liturgies de la présence divine* – the first work of his to become internationally known in the mid-Forties – and his one opera, more like a religious pageant, *Saint François d'Assisi*, which took him nine years to compose and takes six hours to perform. It was first staged at the Paris Opera in 1983 (Ozawa conducted).

Messiaen has played the organ all his life; his regular improvisations at L'Eglise de la Trinité in Paris since he was appointed in 1931 have been a source of wonder. One of his first organ pieces, *Le banquet céleste* (1928), showed that at 20 he arrived fully armed (if Minerva is the appropriate goddess to invoke for such a peaceful saint-like person) with all the harmonic, melodic and metric distinctions, as well as the individuality that makes his music immediately recognizable.

Perhaps it was as well that in World War II Messiaen was captured by the Germans as soon as he became, at least in theory, 'combatant'. In a prisoner of war camp he wrote an hour long quartet for himself and fellow prisoners who happened to be a violinist, a clarinettist and a cellist: *Quatuor pour la fin du temps*. On his release he became a teacher at the Paris Conservatoire, teaching harmony, analysis, and composition. His influence has been considerable, as may be inferred from the list of his pupils, who have included Boulez, Stockhausen, Xenakis, Barraqué and Goehr.

Messiaen is one of the great composers of our time. He has enriched the stores of vocal, organ, piano, chamber and orchestral music; he has also been the chief introducer of that curious instrument, the Ondes Martenot, with electrically invoked sounds that can wail like a banshee or plead like a tender science-fiction creature.

Messiaen is now the Grand Old Man of music – French music in particular – but that doesn't mean that he is unapproachable. Like most saints, the *Maître* has a streak of gaiety within; he is humane, kind, thoughtful and loyal.

In Utah there is a mountain named after him.

YVONNE LORIOD

B. 1924 HOUILLES

Yvonne Loriod studied with Messiaen, and she plays and has recorded practically each and every note for piano that he has written, most of it composed with her and her truly formidable technique in mind. She plays mostly contemporary music and has given all 'his' premières and also many of works by Barraqué, Boulez and Jolivet, as well as concertos by Bartók and Schönberg. In addition she is a teacher of great reputation.

Messiaen's first wife was an invalide and eventually died. Before he was able to marry Yvonne, there poured out of Messiaen those few works in his oeuvre that are not inspired by God or his winged creatures. They are inspired, surely, by love: the unaccompanied choral *Cinq rechants* and the vast *Turangalila-symphonie* (1948).

Two unforgettable experiences were to hear Yvonne alone playing his *Vingt regards sur l'enfant Jesus*, or to hear her and the *Maître* playing on two pianos his *Visions de l'Amen*; like much of Messiaen's *oeuvre*, this is melodic, tonal music shot through with colours richer than the rainbow, life-enhancing for those that can cope with occasional spots of banality, and – there are few brevities among the breviaries – life-lengthening, ecstatic works.

Does not Madame sometimes resemble one of God's feathered creatures? There is, after all, a bird – it is the title of one of his piano pieces – called the Loriot.

MAURICE GENDRON

B. 1920 NICE

At the age of 25, the handsome fair-haired Gendron made his début in London, cutting a dash with his looks, backed up by playing of a high order, in cello sonatas with no less a person than Benjamin Britten at the piano. That same year he made his first concerto appearance in the British capital playing Prokofiev's *Cello Concerto* with the London Philharmonic Orchestra. The association with Britten continued with appearances at the Aldeburgh Festival in Suffolk. On the other side of England, Gendron played in chamber music and with orchestra at the Bath Festival where Yehudi Menuhin directed and led. Later Gendron entered the conducting ring, living for a time in the south of England and directing the Bournemouth Sinfonietta. He has made many excellent recordings of classical and modern French music, among them the Boccherini and Haydn *Concertos*, conducted, no less, by Casals. In conversation Gendron shows, as does his music-making, erudition and a gently teasing wit.

RUGGIERO RICCI

B. 1918 SAN BRUNO, CALIFORNIA

'Woodrow Wilson Rich' it says on his passport, but the photo looks more like Ruggiero Ricci. His trombone-playing Italian father got fed up with being called Ricki and decided to americanize as neo-patriotically as possible. RR began as a child prodigy: San Francisco, New York, London (with Hamilton Harty and the LSO) followed by the other capital cities of Europe. Germany took to him greatly and he made his first 78 records there, which I remember being incredibly impressed by in the early days of World War II – Paganini, Rachmaninov's *Vocalise* and the like.

RR got called up and since he often played at hospitals and camps with no piano he explored the *solo* violin repertoire, which he still likes so much that he gives whole unaccompanied recitals of Bach, Paganini, Prokofiev, Hindemith, Ysaÿe, Wieniawski, Kreisler – there's a lot more of it than you'd think.

Only Heifetz had as much command of as much of the violin as Ricci, which implies that there are certain areas of virtuosity that certain violinists do not care to enter. Ricci has himself spoken of the stigma of virtuosity as though it were something socially unacceptable. It was that stigma that caused instrumentalists to play nothing but sonatas, eschewing the virtuoso pieces that are so often the best performances in the programme. Fortunately there are signs that most of that highbrow nonsense is over and Ruggiero is the man to have around. Not that he doesn't play sonatas and concertos magnificently – he does – but he is one of the two or three most dazzling virtuosi of the violin; moreover he has a light touch with a light piece (as Heifetz had) and a way of making a tune glow and touch your heart.

Wizened faces like his can be seen in many Italian country places but there is nowhere in the world where you will find the equal of his wizard fingers.

CLAUDIO ABBADO

B. 1933 MILAN

'I can never put into words what music is to me, but whatever I do, whatever I say, is *about* it,' Abbado once said to a reporter. And when he was appointed principal conductor of the London Symphony Orchestra, his speech of acceptance at the reception was: 'You see, I don't like to speak; I prefer to conduct.' Those are two of Claudio's *longer* speeches. A more typical utterance was one reported from Vienna: he stopped the orchestra while they were rehearsing Schubert and said, 'Why?' That was all, and it was enough.

Abbado is practically the Harpo of the conducting world – but without the jokes. Which doesn't mean that he hasn't a sense of humour. He is a warm, shy, reserved person, the least ruthless, ego-ridden conductor you can imagine. He is ambitious, but only for music and for bringing music to people – as many as possible (workers to La Scala, for example, in their thousands). The extraordinary thing is that without raising his voice, without ambition, without wheeling and dealing, without saying one word more than he has to, with gestures as beautiful as they are economical, Abbado has risen to some of the highest positions in the musical world: the LSO as mentioned, musical director of La Scala for many years, and now – in the hot seat – musical director of the Vienna Opera.

I first saw this great little man when he went to direct the first session of the European Community Symphony Orchestra in Holland. For two weeks everyone lived in a symphony they had probably never encountered before: Mahler's *Sixth*. It was a life-enhancing experience, even for us onlookers, let alone for the young instrumentalists. Claudio was the leader on the rostrum, but also friend, father, brother to all those teenagers, talking maybe fifteen per cent more than usual, but concerned with every detail. Not just musical details but their recreation, their worries, loneliness or anxiety, bad news from home, illness, were they getting the right food? Nothing was too much trouble for him and his care was shown in the most unobtrusive way. Abbado was almost saint-like with them; and the performance at the Concertgebouw was an overwhelming experience.

One day Claudio had to be away and the orchestra decided to play a trick on him at the final rehearsal. Just before the end of the Mahler symphony there is a long, quiet passage interrupted by a fortissimo chord. The assistant conductor rehearsed the orchestra *not* to play that chord; it took time because either somebody forgot, or some wag couldn't resist blowing a raspberry or something. Came the final rehearsal, they went right through the symphony and when they arrived at that chord there was total silence. Every eye was focussed on Claudio: two things happened. First, with the shock of hearing *nothing* after he had prepared this earthshaking explosion of sound, Abbado *fell over*; secondly, as he picked himself up from the ground, the practical musician in him asked: 'How long did it take you to prepare that?'

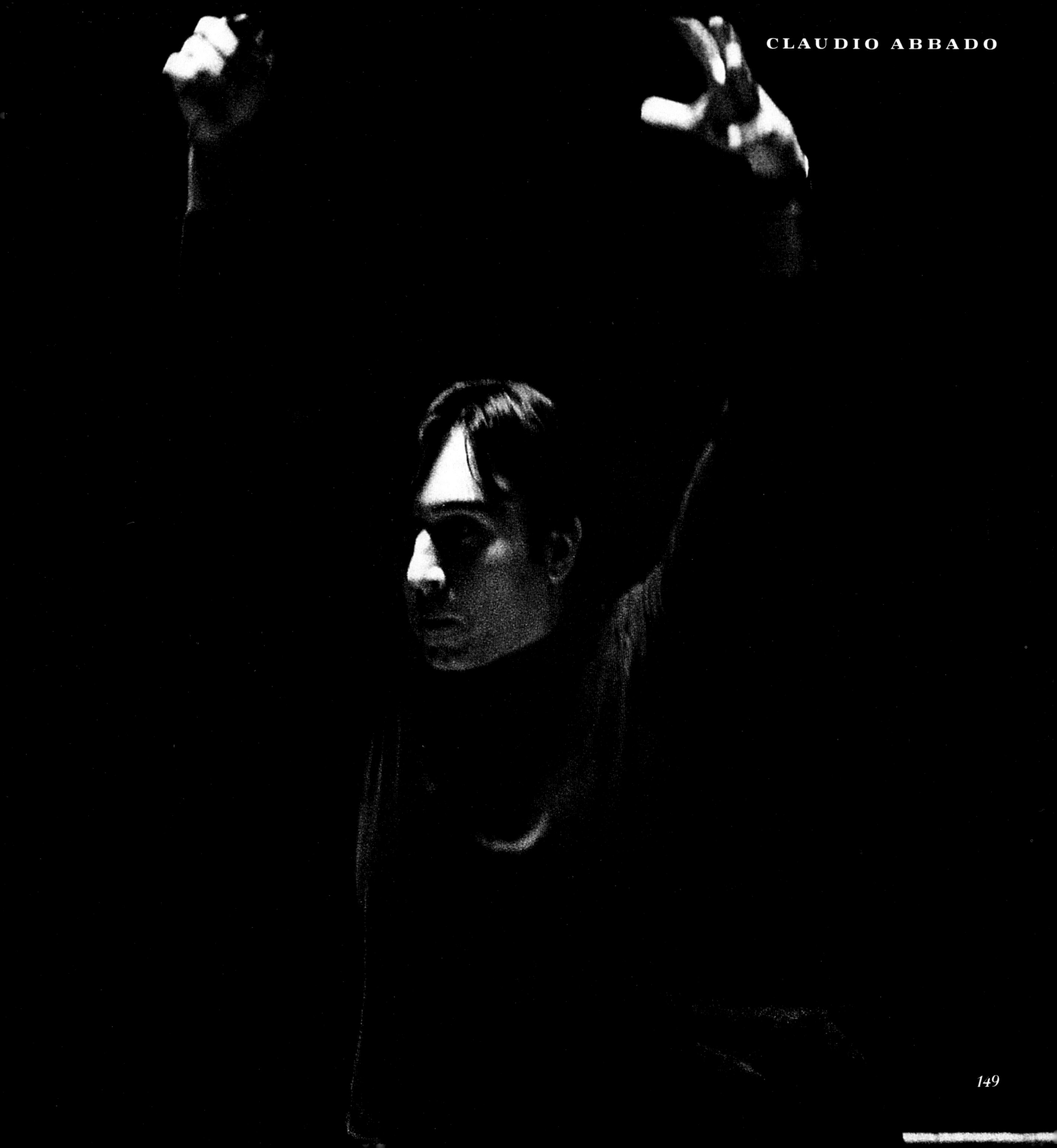

SZYMON GOLDBERG

B. 1909 WLOCLAWEK

Goldberg always reminded me of a nice, friendly Tiger Tim, and almost seemed too unassertive to be a great virtuoso (which he wasn't). What he was, though, was a great musician who played the classical concertos (Haydn, Mozart) exquisitely, thoughtfully and without any hint of the romantic. He brought the same qualities to his pre-war recordings of the Mozart *Violin Sonatas* with Lili Kraus, and to a post-war set with Radu Lupu.

He was a pupil of Carl Flesch, became leader of the Dresden (1925) and then of the Berlin Philharmonic from 1929 until '34. Everybody said he was the best leader that the BPO had this century. During that time he played string trios with Hindemith and Feuermann – their recording of the viola player's *Trio* (1933) is an eloquent tribute to all concerned, not least to the now underrated composer.

Goldberg was captured in Java by the Japanese in 1942 and remained a prisoner of war for two and a half years. He later settled in London, still later in the States. Szymon was conductor of the Netherlands Chamber Orchestra for 20 and more happy years of music-making, encouraging and teaching the young. He was also director of the Manchester Camerata from 1977-'79 after which time his heart began to trouble him more and more, restricting his activities.

He was a fine raconteur and his beloved wife was a good listener and partner. One day, however, following a concert at Dartington, he and I both noticed that after one story there was no laughter, only a look of amazement on her face.

'What's the matter, darling, don't you like my story?'

'Ja, the story is fine,' she said.

'Then what is troubling you?' he asked.

'Only that I never heard it before.'

ANDRÉ PREVIN

B. 1929, BERLIN

By the mid-1960's the name of André Previn was known to at least 90 per cent of the population of Britain, even, I found, to a miner in Cornwall and a cleaning lady in the Highlands. The BBC were plugging *André Previn's Music Night* – the little guy with the American accent certainly had charisma – and the London Symphony were doing all right in reflected glory. But this kind of exposure and popularity inevitably brings reaction; typewriter and armchair critics cannot believe that an idol isn't hollow. The *New York Times* once headlined: 'CAN ANDRÉ PREVIN SUCCEED DE-SPITE SUCCESS?' That says it all. But look: in 1979 the Vienna Philharmonic asked Previn to play Mozart Concertos from the piano with them; in the early 1980's they also asked him to record all the Richard Strauss tone-poems. Did that august, died-in-the-wool con-servative institution know what it was doing, did it need publicity?

It has been a life of changing fortune and music since the infant Andreas Ludwig Priwin played with the infant Gerhard Hoffnung in Berlin in the early Thirties. Paris followed, then California; soon he was playing at jazz sessions, his parents waiting for him to take him home – he was too young to drive or be left out at night, but the money was useful. Sometimes, after school, he would be doing two kinds of homework: school studies and work for the film studios, where he had got a job as an arranger and orchestrator. He remembers the first film score he was allowed to *compose*: 'It was a gift because nobody spoke much – the stars were Jeannette McDonald and Lassie.' At the studios he conducted his own music and an old, old desire, born years back in Berlin when he heard Furtwängler and the Berlin Phil, welled up again. Sensibly, he slogged away with fifth-rate orchestras a lot, learning his craft and biding his time, conducting all-Gershwin pro-grammes. He took lessons with Pierre Monteux which helped him enormously. Monteux was old, wise and wily: 'Alors, you went to 'ear

154

Bernstein last night évidemment, now do it again properly,' 'André. the orchestre play that 'aydn finale ver' well; why don't you leave them alone?'

Finally, Houston engaged André and then there was no stopping him: London Symphony 1968-79, Pittsburgh '76-'86 and he's a regular now with the Royal Phil, and music director with Los Angeles as well as 'guesting' around.

I wish André wasn't such a 'workaholic'. There is something that drives him to accept too much work. Mind you, all these famous conductors are the same (except perhaps Giulini and Kleiber), they *cannot* resist the temptation to conduct, they *get* hooked. But André has shown signs recently of fatigue in his music-making. There are more than glimpses of the old superb, but I think he should watch it . . . for *our* sakes. Because he is damn good, he makes music live for you, whether it's Mozart or Vaughan Williams, Rachmaninoff, Debussy or Gershwin (his record on which he plays and conducts the *Concerto in F* is still the tops). And his own compositions are not so bad, either. I really like that *Guitar Concerto*.

ALEXANDER TCHEREPNIN

B. 1899 ST PETERSBURG, D. 1977 PARIS

He had the misfortune to compose the work that everybody wanted to play, have a record of, hear him play, have another record of, when he was in his teens. His father Nicolai, also a composer, wrote the first original score for Diaghilev, a ballet, *Le Pavillon d'Armide*.

Tcherepnin Non Papa studied with Liadov (who *nearly* wrote *The Firebird*), then went to Paris. There his piano teacher/mentor, Isidore Philippe looked at his many teenage pieces, sorted them arbitrarily into groups and said (according to Sasha): 'These you will call *Feuillets d'album*, these *Capriccios*, these *Songs without Words*, and these . . . these you will call *Bagatelles*!' And it was those *Bagatelles opus 5* that hit the jackpot. Why? The composer never knew. He scored a minor success with his first *Symphony* in 1927 partly because its scherzo was scored for percussion alone. Later he developed a theory of limited serialism, based on a nine-note scale, but, although he composed a lot of music, he tended to remain a 'first performance' composer.

He travelled a lot in Japan and China, taught many composers there in the mid-Thirties and brought back a Chinese pianist wife, a lady of some charm, and enormous tenacity where furthering her husband's music was concerned.

Sasha was tall, and somewhat elegant, despite limbs that seemed too long, or was it that he was always stooping to talk to his little wife Ming and their two composer sons? He had great charm, much learning, was multi-lingual and rather diffident, except when he gave a lecture during which words positively cascaded out of him with the typical Russian guttural 'ch' sound on every 'h' and a total lack of articles, definite or indefinite. I can see his friendly face now and I can hear those intriguing, gem-hard *Bagatelles*.

NATHAN MILSTEIN

B. 1904 ODESSA

We tend to think of Milstein and Horowitz as in some ways older than they really are, forgetting that they left Russia *after*, not *before*, the Revolution. In fact they left Russia together as a violin and piano duo, after having done quite a bit of touring at home between 1922-5. It was on Christmas Eve 1925 that the pair left Soviet Russia with the blessing of the authorities, their first call being the Russian Embassy in Paris. They had their first great success in Spain and from there they were booked for a lengthy tour in South America. Following this, Milstein went his own way, making a crucial début with the Philadelphia Orchestra and Stokowski in 1929. It was 14 years before he became an American citizen, but by then he had travelled the length and breadth of the continent. In 1932 he made his début in Britain, playing the Brahms and Tchaikovsky concertos; strange that fifty years later he is living in London, (*mirabile dictu*, within a bow's length or two of Yehudi Menuhin; I see them both when I do my shopping in Belgravia).

The British public has never quite made up its mind about Milstein; elsewhere he is accepted without any hesitation as one of the world's three or four absolute masters; but in the UK, whilst his fantastic – *still* fantastic – command of the instrument is taken for granted, there are some who blow hot and cold as to whether Milstein is a hot (passionate, full of heart) or cold (intellectual or merely virtuosic) violinist. So Milstein very sensibly does not give London much of a chance to make up its mind. Nor does he acquiesce in the general opinion that our capital is the musical hub of the world. On the contrary, he thinks that London, like New York, is just an enormous musical supermarket. Sharp grapes?

PIERRE BOULEZ

B. 1925 MONTBRISON

'The career is more interesting than the music,' Virgil Thomson once remarked about Pierre Boulez. That sounds as though it may be putting down Boulez' compositions, but it may be true, or at any rate true for this century. What has Boulez done for music? He has given us two or three extraordinary, epoch-making compositions; he has performed an important evangelical job as a conductor of twentieth-century music and, for the last decade, he has been creating the right conditions for the music of the next few decades to emerge.

Boulez began by providing music for Jean-Louis Barrault's theatre in Paris; a series of connected concerts, *'Domaine Musicale'*, provided Paris audiences in the Fifties with an opportunity of hearing music of the Second Viennese School and young contemporary composers including, of course, works by himself like *Le marteau sans maître*. Dissatisfied with the standard of orchestral performances of twentieth-century works and seeing no younger men who would or could conduct this music with energy, conviction and clarity, Boulez leapt into the arena. Initially he made one or two misguided attempts at Beethoven and Wagner. He became principal guest conductor for the BBC in '64, their chief conductor from '71-'75, guest conductor at the Cleveland '69-'70, and chief conductor for the New York Phil from '71-'77. New York was not as receptive as London, but in both places the change in programming and performance of twentieth-century music has been very considerably for the better.

Boulez had left France in disgust at ministerial diffidence but returned in '76 to direct IRCAM (*L'Institut de Recherche et de la Co-ordination Acoustique-Musique*). Boulez believes that new materials in music are now as necessary as they were at the beginning of this century in architecture when glass, steel and concrete brought in change. His own *Répons*, originally composed in 1981 but subsequently varied and added to (as with most of his later works), has gone a long way to justify IRCAM.

Boulez does not suffer fools or incompetence, but he is no bogey-man. On the contrary he is modest, generous, charming and extremely considerate. Two typical quotes: 'Sixty per cent of my activity is to do with a lot of people, so I long to have forty per cent to myself to compensate; so whenever I can, I put myself in confinement.' And, to a journalist who asked him if he had ever been in love: 'That has happened, yes. One cannot say it has happened often.'

ALFRED BRENDEL

B. 1931 WIESENBERG

Ken Dodd and Alfred Brendel both have a lot of teeth showing and they both have a sense of humour. Alfred used to give recitals with the baritone Hermann Prey and one of their ways of banishing boredom when waiting at German railway junctions was to make faces in those four-shot photographic booths you find on platforms, acting out a line from *Schöne Müllerin* or *Winterreise*. Another favourite used to be misprints: Alfred would hand you the latest from his wallet and scan your face eagerly until you had got the point, then he would explode with laughter.

This side of his character is not obvious as the pianist hurtles on to the platform like a greyhound out of a trap, eager to get his grip on us and the music; he hates waiting in the artists' room. Just occasionally there will be a time when Alfred thinks too much and playing a simple tune may become too self-conscious, but by and large he is the essence and spirit of any music he has played, and, it follows, thought deeply about for many years. The balance between head and heart is perfect; he will enjoy the virtuoso element if the music calls for that, but in the performance you will not be aware of technical problems. On the other hand, particularly in late Beethoven, you will be aware of the struggle and the wrestling with the material. Playing Haydn, Mozart, Schubert, Weber (his record of the *Konzertstück* is like a dream of romance, wonderfully abetted by Abbado's conducting), Liszt, Schönberg, Busoni – he is one of the great artists of our time. I once sat next to Alfred for a late night Edinburgh Festival concert in which Stomu Yamashta improvised for half-an-hour on about ninety percussion instruments. When it finally came to an end, Alfred said: 'He reminds me of a little dog in a forest; he cannot bear to pass a single tree. . .'

CLAUDIO ARRAU

B. 1903 CHILE

Amazing to think that he first played in London in 1922. What is it about his playing that is so compelling? Maybe it is the mixture of the Teutonic training and the Latin temperament. From the age of eight Arrau studied in Germany, making his début in Berlin at eleven, winning the Geneva Grand Prix at 24. Since then he has never, as they say, looked back. At the age of 33 he played all Bach's keyboard works in the German capital. For many he is *the* interpreter of Beethoven, Chopin, Liszt, Schumann and Brahms, not forgetting Mozart. He has also taught a great deal and his pupils have all adored him.

IGOR OISTRAKH

B. 1931 ODESSA

Igor was born shortly before his father and his pianist mother moved to Moscow where David had been appointed lecturer. David not only begat Igor, he taught him too, and when the time came they played and recorded the Bach *Double Concerto*. They also played Mozart's *Sinfonia Concertante* together with the son on the violin and the father on the viola. Curiously, Igor's official London début took place a year before his father's, an example of Soviet inconsistency. The previous year Igor had won the Wieniawski Prize in Warsaw (his father managed only second prize back in the Thirties). As his father before him, Igor now teaches in Moscow, and gives concerts in the West and in America.

DAVID OISTRAKH

B. 1908 ODESSA, D. 1974 AMSTERDAM

David Oistrakh was one of the many outstanding musicians whose appearances in the West were delayed much too long by the Soviet authorities and World War II. Although he had won prestigious prizes in '37, it was '53 before London and Paris heard him, and '55 before he reached New York. By that time he was a legend. What came true, though, was his playing and his character, both noble; he had virtuosity enough and to spare, as his performance of the Khachaturian *Concerto* showed, but it was his heartfelt lyricism and sense of style that made his audience adore his Mozart, Beethoven and Brahms. Of his compatriots, Prokofiev infused the spirit of his dedicatee so deeply in his *F minor Sonata*, and Shostakovich even more deeply in the *Violin Concerto No. 1* (also dedicated to Oistrakh). In later years joint recitals with Richter brought great joy, as with everything the man did.

Overworked though he was, Oistrakh always found time to teach and he was mentor and guide to his students in quite the old way of master and pupil. He was a gentle man and a gentleman, and one of the supreme violinists of all time.

Yehudi Menuhin once asked Oistrakh why he did not come to live in the West. His answer: 'I owe the state everything. They are responsible for my upbringing and have seen to it that I have had the best musical education and training. My family are there. It would be disloyal of me to live elsewhere.'

Someone once asked him: 'What is the most difficult piece you play?' Typically, Oistrakh answered: 'I don't play the most difficult pieces.'

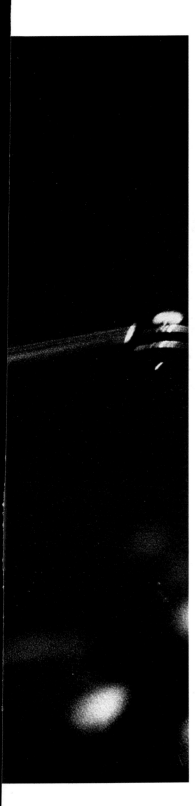

SIR YEHUDI MENUHIN

B. 1916 NEW YORK

We owe him a lot in England and it is nice that he finally decided to take English citizenship (although he still has American too) so that we can call him Sir Yehudi and the Queen could grant him the Order of Merit. Yehudi is a great man, has done wonderfully by the human race, can sometimes say what needed to be said, can make music to touch the heart and please the mind, and has educated a lot of children to be good musicians.

Who else, after the Nine Days War, would have had the imagination, compassion and sheer nerve to go and play charity concerts for the Arabs as well as the Jews?

In his teens Yehudi's playing had about it an element of the miraculous. How else explain the profound maturity that was part of

the playing of this child? Many events in his life have become part of the Menuhin legend: not being allowed to cross the road by himself until he was well past puberty; the 16-year-old playing the Elgar *Concerto* with the adoring old composer conducting; the lad being shocked when the elderly Toscanini, on being disturbed at a piano rehearsal, wrenched the whole telephone apparatus out of the wall; YM at six o'clock in the morning playing to Georges Enesco as he packed his bags for a journey in the hope of persuading the Romanian violinist to give him lessons; after a few years Enesco passing his young charge on to the more disciplined Protestant German violinist.

Adolf Busch, thinking that YM was getting too wayward and passionate in his playing; YM playing Bartók to Bartók in such a way that the composer exclaimed that he thought a composer had to be long dead for his music to be performed like that; YM with Benjamin Britten as his pianist playing recitals in the newly opened concentration camps. Why do we knock Yehudi for having a go at jazz with Stephane Grappelli and Indian music with Ravi Shankar? What a great 'crossover', in both cases how touching and instructive the results! Music is so often a matter of giving and loving and communicating – like life itself – hasn't Yehudi done his share of that?

CARLO MARIA GIULINI

B. 1914 BARLETTA, ITALY

There is an aura about Giulini, something almost saintly. He has never had to worry about discipline with orchestras, he is a man you want instinctively to serve, to follow. This is partly because he never does anything except serve the composers he permits himself to conduct. His repertoire is small because he will not conduct a work or a composer with whom he does not feel in tune. He won't conduct all the year round; he needs time to think, he says. He won't conduct unless conditions are good; for many years he didn't conduct opera because he found conditions in the opera house were unsuitable. He is fortunate, of course, that he is able to afford to bide his time; but his principles are so sound that he would do what he felt was right even if he were poor.

Giulini is concerned with the mysteries of life and death, the mysteries of man and music. He is also deeply religious. Perhaps that is why he needs, and takes, time to think.

Giulini began life as a viola player in the Augusteo Orchestra in Rome, enjoying playing under the world's greatest conductors and learning from them. When the mighty Victor de Sabata had to give up the musical direction of La Scala, Milan for health reasons, his assistant Giulini took over. He also began his long association with the Holland Festival in the Fifties, as well as with the Edinburgh Festival and the Philharmonia Orchestra. In 1958 came the Visconti production of Verdi's *Don Carlos* that many of us remember as the finest post-war performance at Covent Garden. Giulini's performances of the same composer's *Requiem* and *Four Sacred Pieces* were also unforgettable. From '69 to '72 Giulini was in Chicago and from '78 to '84 in Los Angeles.

Giulini is a joy to meet, a man of perfect courtesy, serious, simple, interested in people. It was rather strange with such a man to find that he relaxes by watching westerns and that, in another life, he would like to play jazz piano.

SIR COLIN DAVIS

B. 1927 WEYBRIDGE

These are rather early photographs of Colin. I have one or two snaps of him at home, looking like this: making funny faces as he is perplexed by what is happening. He is either not sure if he has made a mess himself, or he cannot believe that the players could make such a mess of it; he is the conductor and therefore he is responsible, but he doesn't want to be a boss and bawl them out. Colin always took to the music more than he did to leadership. He was bright enough to see this and to force himself eventually to take up the challenge of leadership.

In the late 1940's there was a group of players and singers who got together; first of all it was called after an oboe player called Kalmar. I remember taking part in a performance of the *St Matthew Passion* in a studio in Holland Park in West London. There was only room for a handful of players and the solo singers on the floor; we in the minute chorus were mostly in rows on a couple of bunks. It was a bit like the cabin scene in the Marx Brothers film *A Night at the Opera*. Various people had a shot at directing a Kalmar performance; this time it was a young clarinettist called Colin Davis. (Maybe the soprano was April Cantelo; she would be Colin's first wife and they would have two children, but that was in the future.) In 1949 the Kalmar went to Bryanston to the Summer School of Music; Roger Desormière did most of the conducting, Colin played clarinet but conducted a little. The next year he started conducting some of the performances of the Chelsea Opera Group, which included the Kalmar members. *Don Giovanni* was the first opera Colin did; others included *Idomeneo*, *Zäide* (in which I sang solo!) and an inspiring *Trojans*; these were the first of memorable Davis performances of Mozart and Berlioz.

Colin turned professional by landing a job as assistant conductor of the BBC Scottish Orchestra, where he was able to learn some repertoire. The big breakthrough came in 1959 when he substituted for Klemperer in a concert performance of *Don Giovanni* at the Royal Festival Hall. From that moment he never looked back, although there were some times of despair. He met those challenges: Sadler's Wells in the early sixties, the BBC Symphony Orchestra later, musical director of Covent Garden '71-'86. During the Covent Garden period there was time to 'guest' and to form lasting associations in Boston and Amsterdam. In London there were fine Mozart performances: *Idomeneo*, *Clemenza di Tito*.

Another lasting relationship has been with the Bavarian Radio Symphony Orchestra, and since leaving the Royal Opera House Sir Colin (he was knighted in 1980) has become music director. He retains a house in the English countryside, however, and he still remains a very private man, content, when he is able, to spend all his time with Shamsi, his Persian wife, together with the five children of his second marriage. No distractions: just a simple life, enjoying his family, books, and music.

TRISTAN FRY

B. 1946 LONDON

Tristan is a hit and *stay* man, leading a life of calculated violence done to many percussion instruments. He started off in the London Philharmonic Orchestra and was a founder member of the Nash Ensemble and of the Pierrot Players which Harrison Birtwistle and Peter Maxwell Davies started (later to arise phoenix-like from a percussive episode to become the Fires of London).

Tristan proved invaluable at a time when the percussion department in such chamber groups was adding to its resources, complications and virtuosity with composers that TF worked with, such as Taverner, Gerhard, the two English composers mentioned above, and Bruno Maderna. Pierre Boulez was lucky to have Tristan for the local première of *Le marteau sans maître*. In between playing that kind of date, Tristan might have been found playing for Danny Kaye, Bing Crosby, Frank Sinatra and Jack Benny; at the Proms one day playing Bartók and Stockhausen, with the Basie or Ellington remnant bands the next, and then back to being the regular timpanist of the Academy of St Martin's. He is also a founder member of the group Sky, together with John Williams.

A genial, friendly, brilliant timpanist and percussionist. A shrewd business man too.

GEZA ANDA

B. 1921 BUDAPEST, D. 1976 ZURICH

Geza Anda was always more willing to talk of his master Erno von Dohnanyi than himself; how the Master's memory had stored all of Beethoven, Mozart, Brahms, and Schumann and so on, and yet each time he played there would be one slip which Dohnanyi would handle in remarkable ways: if his memory slipped during the exposition of a sonata movement he would elaborate something that he would later improvise in again in the style of that composer in the development, and then include it also in the re-capitulation. This was really creative musicianship, said Geza, and he would tell all *his* pupils in case they should find themselves in the same predicament. Geza also told me how Dohnanyi once played a 'different' *Fughetta* in Schumann's *Scenes of Childhood*. On Geza inquiring the provenance of the new fughetta in the artists' room afterwards, Dohnanyi admitted that he had forgotten how the fughetta went but knew there should be one at that point, so he made one up – in the style of Schumann, naturally.

Geza lived for his Master's memory and was always trying to emulate him, though not, he explained, by having memory losses. These Geza Anda did not have, in my experience. My experience with him was of faultless Mozart directed from the keyboard, spirited Bartók, and excellent Brahms and Beethoven for which he was famous on two continents.

After winning the coveted Liszt Prize, Anda escaped to Switzerland in 1943, becoming a citizen of that country in '55. He died of cancer much too young, mourned by his friends and colleagues.

SEIJI OZAWA

B. 1935 MANCHURIA

There is no doubt that Ozawa inspires real affection and, yes, love in the musicians he works with. I first saw something of this in Hong Kong where he was conducting the NHK Tokyo: the whole orchestra plus some wives and children were at the airport, plane delayed. I was interviewing Ozawa so I tailed him as he went round talking to groups of his players. It was like Henry V going round the camp before Agincourt.

In March '86 he conducted Messiaen's *St François* with the BBC. For four days he had separate sectional rehearsals; they didn't but *he* worked nine hours a day; then there were general rehearsals, for several days; Ozawa was always as fresh as a daisy, inspiring, friendly, knowing when to stop, when to trust that the players would get it right next time. And right from the first he had the whole of this vast score in his head. Again, the players said they really loved him.

Brought up partly in China, partly in his native Japan, Ozawa had a difficult time. There was no money in the family, and the Japanese were used to 'foreign' conductors not native ones. He managed to get to France, entered and won a competition at Besançon where, as luck would have it, Charles Munch — Ozawa's predecessor at Boston — happened to be on the jury. Invited to Boston's music summer camp, Tanglewood, Bernstein took a shine to him and made him assistant at the New York Philharmonic. In the meantime there were classes with Karajan, Toronto 1964-70, then San Francisco, and now Boston, where he has been director since 1973. From Boston he 'guests' in Berlin, and at La Scala; he has done *Cosi fan tutte* at Salzburg, *Eugène Onegin* at Covent Garden, *Fidelio* and *Elektra* at the Paris Opera as well as the aforementioned *St François*.

You can see how disciplined he is, how deeply serious and committed, how intelligent, how human, how loving . . .

AARON COPLAND

B. 1900 BROOKLYN

I once asked: 'How is it that a Jewish kid from Brooklyn, first generation American, can write music that everybody recognizes as belonging to the great American outdoors?'

Copland replied, 'It could have something to do with the well-known Jewish/American adaptability – or maybe it could have to do with the wide intervals and the spaced chords that I frequently use in my music.'

Copland's father came from Eastern Europe and on his arrival at Ellis Island an immigration officer mistakenly wrote Copland instead of Kaplan and refused to change it. He soon became reasonably well off in Brooklyn and was able to send his son abroad to study music, to Paris, in 1921. Aaron couldn't think of any famous composer who had studied with a woman but nevertheless he went to Nadia Boulanger. When he had completed his studies Boulanger indicated her confidence in him by getting him a commission to write a *Symphony* for organ and orchestra which she premièred in New York. When the last chord was dying down the conductor turned to the audience and said: 'A young man who can write music like that at twenty-three will be ready in five years' time to commit murder.' Harsh words – wonderful publicity.

Jazzy pieces gave way to austere ones like the masterly *Piano Variations*. A synthesis of the two styles, plus commissions to compose ballets with western or New England settings led to such successes as *Billy the Kid*, *Rodeo* and *Appalachian Spring*. These and the exuberant *El Salon Mexico*, together with frequent performances by his friend Serge Koussevitsky with the Boston Symphony made Copland America's most popular contemporary composer (there are strong parallels with George Gershwin's success in an even more popular style).

Copland taught, lectured, broadcast, played piano in public, and

fought for American music by organizing concerts. founding a maga-
zine and securing performing rights. Conducting came a little later.
enabling him to tour the world as a cultural ambassador. Everybody
likes Aaron. he is always equable. serious yet accessible. I have the
feeling that performing was a compensation as he realized that his
music was getting less active. In his mid-seventies he announced that
he would compose no more. Latterly his short-term memory has de-
serted him with the result that he has had to give up conducting and
appearing in public. But he will happily talk about the past. seated in
his many-windowed studio up the Hudson river. where you have the
comfort of sitting in a booklined room yet feel as if you are in the open
air. among the rhododendrons and the trees. That room could be a
metaphor for his music — fresh. natural. yet with an intellectual core.

SIR CHARLES GROVES

B. 1915 LONDON

During World War II I became aware that the BBC Theatre Orchestra had a most exciting young associate conductor. At the end of some brilliant performance the announcer would say, 'That performance of (whatever it was) was conducted by Charles Groves.' Sometimes he would go on to say 'and that crash you heard was the conductor knocking over a music stand.' Charles then went up to Manchester to the BBC Northern Orchestra, a stalwart bunch of tough cookies. Then for ten years Groves spread his wings with the Bournemouth Symphony, following that with some excellent work

with Welsh National Opera in 1961-3, thence to the Royal Liverpool
Philharmonic (music stands stayed put by this time!) where he did
fine performances of Elgar, Delius, the Busoni *Piano Concerto* and
works by the younger British School such as Britten and Tippett.

He is a loyal man and friend, an excellent companion, especially
when he reminisces about venerable figures of the past, like Thomas
Beecham, with affection and admiration.

The family Groves is a good one to spend time with: Sir Charles
himself (he was knighted in 1973), his supportive wife Hilary, and
two of the children who work in the music world – Jonathan as an
agent, and Sally as composers' friend and ally at the publishers
Schotts.